TAKE
COMMAND

TAKE COMMAND

10 LEADERSHIP PRINCIPLES I LEARNED
IN THE MILITARY AND PUT TO WORK
FOR DONALD TRUMP

———

KELLY PERDEW

WEST POINT GRADUATE AND AIRBORNE RANGER
TURNED ENTREPRENEUR AND WINNER OF "THE APPRENTICE 2"

Since 1947
REGNERY
PUBLISHING, INC.
An Eagle Publishing Company • Washington, DC

Cataloging-in-Publication data on file with the Library of Congress

ISBN 1-59698-000-1

Published in the United States by
Regnery Publishing, Inc.
One Massachusetts Avenue, NW
Washington, DC 20001

www.regnery.com

Distributed to the trade by
National Book Network
Lanham, MD 20706

Manufactured in the United States of America

10 9 8 7 6 5 4 3 2 1

Books are available in quantity for promotional or premium use. Write to Director of Special Sales, Regnery Publishing, Inc., One Massachusetts Avenue NW, Washington, DC 20001, for information on discounts and terms or call (202) 216-0600.

Contents

Foreword by Donald Trump

The *Apprentice* continues to be great fun for me, and a good investment of my time. As a business leader, I am tremendously gratified by the record ratings and high interest in my nationally televised job search. The whole world, it seems, wants to know what it takes to be an executive at The Trump Organization—and I love showing them. During Season 2 I didn't let up on the pressure for a minute. Business doesn't let up, so neither do I.

On the whole, I was very impressed with the caliber of candidates who vied to become my next Apprentice. I took note of Kelly early, and as the show continued I had to admire his progress. He attained record results, volunteering to take the helm as project manager on four occasions, and led his team to victory on all four—a record score card, unbeaten by any of *The Apprentice* candidates to date.

Kelly is quick to credit his West Point education and experience as an Army officer with giving him everything it takes to face any challenge—in business and in life. After seeing him in action, I'd have to agree. While Kelly is unquestionably a leader, his background has also taught him to follow, a very valuable distinction. The most important attribute I could ask for in any employee is a sense of loyalty and duty, and Kelly has both.

When I selected Kelly as my new Apprentice, I offered him the choice of working on a building project either in Las Vegas or New York. He immediately chose New York and moved to Manhattan, because he wanted to work as closely as possible with me. I have given him a number of important tasks, and his progress has been terrific. He is an excellent employee, but his heart is in start-up ventures, and he has also come up with a great new business for us to do together. It's called Trump Direct Media, and it will be coming soon.

In this book, Kelly elaborates on the ten principles he credits for his success, up to and including winning *The Apprentice 2*: Duty. Impeccability. Passion. Perseverance. Planning. Teamwork. Loyalty. Flexibility. Selfless Service. Integrity. He also interviews a number of business icons who share both these characteristics and his military background. I can certainly vouch that he possesses all of these attributes, and has brought them to bear on his work at The Trump Organization. I am pleased to have Kelly as my Apprentice, and he has a lot of inspiring words for all of you seeking success in any endeavor.

—DONALD J. TRUMP

Introduction

Take it from me: Army Rangers always lead the way. I was cast as the "military" character on Donald Trump's incredibly popular show *The Apprentice 2*. After fifteen long weeks it came down to me and a Princeton-educated attorney. In front of millions of viewers Donald Trump chose me as his apprentice. Immediately afterwards, I was bombarded with variations of the same question from almost everyone—people I had known for years and done business with, strangers who had followed the show and stopped me on the street to talk, and of course, the media. Everyone wanted to know: *Do you think your military background helped you win The Apprentice?* And even though my four years at West Point and three years of active duty in the Army ended 12 years ago, the answer was and is an unqualified yes. My military background and training were absolutely crucial factors—not only for winning *The Apprentice*, but for succeeding in every venture I have undertaken since that very influential time in my life.

At first, I was matter-of-fact about it: "Yes, of course, my military training helped a lot." I might mention discipline, attention to detail, showing up on time, and saying "Yes Sir!" and "No Ma'am!" But there is so much more to military leadership training than that. It is a whole process, a mindset, an accumulation of hundreds of lessons. Boiled down they become principles that we learn to apply instinctively.

The more I thought about it, the more I realized that what I learned at West Point and in my subsequent military service centered on ten essential principles for effective leadership. These principles are applicable in the Army, the boardroom, or life—but I learned them at West Point, applied them in Ranger training, as an intelligence officer, and then (after obtaining my law degree and an M.B.A. at UCLA) in the five companies that I have been a part of, as either a founding partner or entrepreneurial manager. Certainly they helped me win the privilege of working for Donald Trump, and they are the very foundation of how I live my life and run my businesses.

The essential principles to take command in business and in life are:

- **Duty**. Do what you're supposed to do, when you're supposed to do it.
- **Impeccability**. If it is worth doing, it is worth doing right.
- **Passion**. Be passionate about what you do, and do what you're passionate about.

- **Perseverance**. It's not the size of the dog in the fight, it's the size of the fight in the dog.
- **Planning**. If you fail to plan, you plan to fail.
- **Teamwork**. There is no "I" in TEAM.
- **Loyalty**. Remain loyal, up, down, and across your organization.
- **Flexibility**. In all aspects of life, the person with the most varied responses wins.
- **Selfless Service**. Give back.
- **Integrity**. Take the harder right over the easier wrong.

These principles sound simple, but it takes discipline, training, and devotion to keep them front and center in everything you do. But if you can achieve that, you can achieve your goals, whatever they are.

Don't just take my word for it. Since my *Apprentice* win, I have spoken with a number of outstanding individuals who excelled both in their military careers *and* in their business lives. You might have heard of them without knowing about their military background:

Roger Staubach

The greatest quarterback Navy ever had, Roger won the Heisman Trophy in his junior year. After graduating from the Naval Academy, he spent four years on active duty, including a tour of Vietnam, before starting his pro football career with the Dallas Cowboys. One of the greatest NFL players of the 1970s, he led the Cowboys to two Super Bowl wins. He retired from pro football in 1979 as the highest rated passer of all time, and was elected to the Pro Football Hall of Fame in

1985. He founded The Staubach Company in the late 1970s to represent users of office, industrial, and retail space. Today the Staubach Company has more than 1,300 employees and 50 nationwide locations and encompasses finance, design, construction, and portfolio management. Roger is dedicated to building his company on his core principles of trust and integrity—which he gained in the U.S. Navy.

James V. Kimsey

After graduating from West Point, Jim Kimsey served three combat tours as an Airborne Ranger—two in Vietnam and one in the Dominican Republic—and was inducted into the Ranger Hall of Fame. He transformed Quantum Computer Services into the giant America Online as its founding CEO. AOL is the nation's best-known provider of interactive online services. In 1996 he became Chairman Emeritus of AOL and now devotes his efforts to philanthropy through the Kimsey Foundation, whose overarching mission is to help disadvantaged young people succeed through education and technology.

Ross Perot

Mr. Perot was class president, chairman of the Honor Committee, and Battalion Commander at the Naval Academy in the early 1950s. He borrowed $1,000 from his wife Margot to start EDS, a one-man data processing company, which he sold to GM in 1984 for $2.5 billion. When he ran for president of the United States, he garnered the highest percentage of the vote for a third-party candidate since Theodore Roosevelt. I think Ross is living proof that if you work hard enough, you can accomplish anything.

Marsha "Marty" Evans

The president and chief executive officer of the Red Cross is, at the time of this writing, doing an amazing job leading the relief efforts following the devastation of Hurricane Katrina. Her twenty-nine-year career in the Navy prepared her well for the challenge of leading the largest and most respected humanitarian aid organization in the United States. Marty did much to expand the professional roles for women in the Navy, and retired in 1998 as a Rear Admiral, one of the few women to reach this rank. Before joining the Red Cross, Marty was the CEO of Girl Scouts of the USA, where she increased membership, brought the level of volunteers to an all-time high, and expanded diversity among its members. During my interview with Marty, I was impressed by her dedication to helping others and her phenomenal ability to devise and execute plans.

Bill Coleman

Growing up in a military family, Bill studied computer science at the U.S. Air Force Academy and served as the Chief of Satellite operations for the Office of the Secretary of Defense. After leaving the military, he rose to head software development for Sun Microsystems before striking out on his own to found BEA Systems, which became the leader in Internet infrastructure software in the nineties and was the fastest software company ever to reach $1 billion in annual sales. He is currently focusing on automating IT operations as the CEO of Cassatt Corp. A brilliant software visionary and hi-tech entrepreneur, he is a noted philanthropist who founded the Coleman Institute, a research organization at the University of Colorado specializing in using computers to help people with cognitive disabilities. Anyone who spends any time with Bill can easily see that he is the ultimate planner.

Pete Dawkins

Pete Dawkins was an outstanding cadet at West Point, serving as first captain and brigade commander of the Corps of Cadets, and president of his class of 1959. He played baseball, was an All-East defenseman and assistant captain of the hockey team, and was captain of the 1958 Army football team—the last Army team to record an undefeated season. In his senior year, he won the Heisman Trophy and the Maxwell Trophy, and was selected as a Rhodes Scholar. He attended Oxford University, and later earned a Ph. D. at Princeton's Woodrow Wilson School. In his distinguished twenty-four-year military career he was Airborne and Ranger qualified, and earned the Distinguished Service Medal, the Legion of Merit, two Bronze stars with V for valor, and three Vietnamese Gallantry Crosses. He retired from the Army at the age of forty-three as a brigadier general. Since that time, Pete has spent twenty-two years in private business, most of it in the financial services industry. His experience has spanned investment banking (Partner at Lehman Brothers); strategy consulting (Managing Partner of Bain & Company); insurance and investment (Chairman/CEO of Primerica Financial Services, Inc.); insurance (Vice Chairman and EVP of Travelers Insurance); and banking (Vice Chairman of the Citigroup Private Bank.) Pete embodies the term "leadership." He has excelled at a remarkably wide range of pursuits. He attributes his drive, sense of integrity and commitment to excellence to his parents, to his midwestern upbringing in Michigan, and to his formative experience at the Military Academy.

Each of these accomplished individuals agrees that the ten core principles taught by the military form the foundation for their success. Hey, even Donald Trump attended a military high school!

These ten principles can work for you too. Whether you're seeking success in a boardroom, on the playing field, on a sales call, fundraising, leading troops in Iraq, or starting your own small business, the principles necessary to take command and be effective are the same.

For you servicemen and women who are preparing to enter the civilian workforce, take heart and be proud of your service. The business world needs your principles and your training! For those of you without a military background, don't worry; these principles are achievable outside the military, and now is the time for you to learn.

CHAPTER ONE

Duty: Do What You're Supposed to Do, When You're Supposed to Do It

Duty was a straightforward concept at our house. Bottom line, it meant doing what I was supposed to without being told to do it. My parents divorced when I was six years old and I lived for the next ten years with my mother in Florida. Then, at fifteen, I decided to live with my dad in Cheyenne, Wyoming. I knew I'd be in college in a few years—and I wanted to get to know my dad better before I left.

In high school, I played football, baseball, tennis, and ran track, but basketball was my true love. My schedule was crammed, but my dad—a successful real estate developer—insisted I find a job on top of everything else. He wanted me to learn what it takes to earn money myself. He had the right idea.

So I got a job at McDonald's and worked after school and on weekends. Over the summer I worked on a ranch. The ranch hands got a good laugh when on my first day of work I showed up wearing a baseball cap, tank top, and sweat pants. They were all dressed in stiff jeans, boots, long-sleeved shirts and rawhide gloves. I realized why after about eight hours of baling hay. When I limped home that first day, blood was running down my arms and thighs. For those of you that have never come in contact with real, cut hay, you have to handle it carefully. It is very sharp.

The farm hands all got a kick out of the city kid working on a ranch, but as the summer progressed I actually got proficient enough to brand cattle. Branding was a team effort: one cowboy sat on the ground and hooked a boot heel behind the calf's back leg to hold its hindquarters, and the other placed a knee on its upper shoulder and held its front leg to further immobilize it. Another ranch hand would brand the calf, give it a shot of medicine to prevent infection, and quickly trim its horns before releasing it back into the herd.

> Duty then is the sublimest word in the English language. You should do your duty in all things. You can never do more, you should never wish to do less.
>
> —GENERAL ROBERT E. LEE

I learned a lot about ranching—it definitely toughened me up, strengthened me for the football season, and taught me respect for ranchers and farmers and the work they do. Actually, between McDonald's and the ranch, I covered a cow's life from birthing to burgers. And I learned what it meant to wake up at 4 a.m. to drive out to the ranch to bale hay all day under the blazing sun, to empty the trash at McDonald's, and to fit work in with sports and academics. Through it all, I didn't want to let anyone down.

Besides impressing upon me the importance of making my own money, my dad, a self-made man, had definite opinions on higher education. He believed it was the student, not the school, who determined the quality of one's education.

I agreed, but I also knew that it was important to create networks for success. No one can do it entirely on his or her own. I knew I could get a great education at the University of Wyoming, but I wanted to be on a fast track with students at Stanford or Harvard. For my junior year, I set up an elaborate chart listing all the pros and cons of various schools. No school even came close to what the U.S. military academy had to offer. So at sixteen, I started networking to make my way through the highly competitive application process.

One day, then-Congressman Dick Cheney was speaking at the cross-town rival high school. I sat through his speech and afterwards introduced myself, telling him that I was interested in attending a military academy. We're all familiar with the saying "It's not what you know, it's who you know." Meeting Dick Cheney certainly helped me. He, of course, later served as secretary of Defense while I was an Army officer, and now he's vice president of the United States. I am a huge believer in networks, in connecting people and helping them out. Mr. Cheney kindly did that for me, providing my official nomination to West Point, the final step of a grueling application process.

I received an early acceptance to West Point during my senior year of high school. Now that I was in, I figured I'd better go see exactly what I was getting myself into. My dad and I flew out to New York, and I spent the night with a cadet in his barracks while my dad stayed in Hotel Thayer on the Army post (and yes, West Point is on an Army post, not a college campus). The cadet escorted me to a lunch formation and I attended several classes. It was a March day on the Hudson River and the weather was freezing cold, gloomy, and gray. But the sheer history and stature of the campus made a tremendous impression on me. The West Point program, which focused on intellectual, physical, military, and moral/ethical training, was very impressive. The weight of history that hung over the almost two-hundred-year-old Army post was awesome.

I was barely eighteen years old, and it was amazing to think that I could receive the same training as Ulysses S. Grant, Robert E. Lee, Douglas MacArthur, Dwight D. Eisenhower, George S. Patton... the famous names went on and on. It was a popular saying at West Point: "Much of the history we teach was made by people we taught." What was most inspiring was that I knew and could see that West Point didn't just provide a great liberal education—it provided real leadership training.

> How can you come to know yourself? Never by thinking, always by doing. Try to do your duty, and you'll know right away what you amount to.
>
> —JOHANN WOLFGANG VON GOETHE

Still, I was facing a huge decision. West Point was hardly your typical run-of-the-mill college experience. Many of my friends from Florida and Wyoming were heading off to schools like Stanford, with outstanding academic reputations, or schools where sports and parties were the primary attraction. I, on the other hand, was committing myself to four years of the most rigorous discipline and training with little freedom, and on top of that, a five-year stint as a United States Army officer after graduation. I was facing duty for the *next nine years*—more than half my life up to that point!

Going to West Point was a decision I have never regretted, not even for a moment. West Point was absolutely the right place for me. The official West Point mission is to educate, train and inspire the corps of cadets so that each graduate is a commissioned leader of character committed to the values of duty, honor, country; and to prepare them for a career of professional excellence and service to the nation as an officer in the United States Army. I give them credit for doing an excellent job.

A key component of duty is *accountability*. That was instilled immediately and forcibly at West Point. As plebes (freshmen) my classmates and I were immediately saddled with all kinds of daunting responsibilities, none of them optional. Life was a blur of classes, drill, sports, studying, and the many other tasks that were assigned to us. We had to do them all, like them or not. It was our duty.

> A duty dodged is like a debt unpaid; it is only deferred, and we must come back and settle the account at last.
>
> —JOSEPH F. NEWTON

Like many of my classmates, I did not miss a single class, not once in four years, for the simple reason that I wasn't allowed to. Roll was taken at the start of every class. There was no such thing as not completing an assignment or failing to turn in homework. This was not at all like regular college, where a student might say, "Oh, I blew off the paper," or "I let that assignment slide." Skipping assignments and taking the "F" was not even within the realm of possibility. It just did not happen. We actually attended classes and learned the material.

Then, of course, there was our military training, which included everything from tactical training to parade or "drill" exercises. For much of the year parades were held for the public who came by to see what West Point is all about. We were told that parades were an excellent way to build discipline and attention to detail: preparing our uniforms, being inspected, marching with precision, and standing in formation for hours in the heat, cold, or rain. Endless hours of standing still in hot wool uniforms or—later in the year, walking in circles in the rain with icy winds blowing off the river—sure wasn't fun. It was a leadership challenge simply motivating everyone to do it!

Rollcall was taken at every drill formation, and just like class, there was no such thing as being unaccounted for. At West Point, as in the Army, there were no missing persons. If someone didn't answer roll-call, another cadet was sent to find him or her and escort them to class or formation. There was literally no place to hide. A cadet might be really sick and legitimately need to see the doctor, but he or she would be tracked down and his or her whereabouts noted. We were training to be soldiers, the most serious job in the world, and accountability for every person was critical. You can't go to war and succeed without your full unit.

In the bigger picture, the whole idea behind going to West Point is doing your duty for your country. General MacArthur gave a very famous speech to the cadets at West Point in 1962 when he accepted the Thayer Award for his distinguished service. He was in his eighties at the time, and his stirring message served as his farewell address. General MacArthur spoke eloquently about "those three hallowed words: duty, honor, country," in one of the most inspirational speeches ever. As cadets we were trained and prepared to make the ultimate sacrifice for our country, to put ourselves in harm's way, and to remember that when we gave or were given orders, they could involve life and death.

The United States Army is a volunteer organization. Yes, there have been drafts to shore up the ranks in the past, but since my cadet days, it's been an all-volunteer force. And it's the strongest, greatest, and most effective fighting force in the world. Men and women who volunteer for the Army learn duty as a first principle. They center their lives on it. While West Point offers an excellent education and the army offers great training, programs, and a chance to see the world, the cadets and soldiers who step up and volunteer do it for duty's sake.

When you think of duty, you immediately think of the military—and men like Roger Staubach. Staubach was drafted by the Dallas Cowboys in 1964, but completed his military service, including a tour in Vietnam, before starting his pro career. He didn't join the Cowboys until 1969—as a twenty-seven-year-old rookie. As a Heisman-Trophy winner, Roger Staubach could have argued that he could do a better job representing the Navy as a football star rather than serving in Vietnam. But he didn't even consider it. He went to do his duty.

> By learning to obey, you will know how to command.
>
> —ITALIAN PROVERB

Roger told me, "When I was in high school I went to visit the Naval Academy and really liked it. The mixture of discipline, solid education, and outstanding sports program just felt right to me. I was eligible for the pro football draft after my junior year, because I had spent a year at junior college before entering the Naval Academy, but I knew that I still had five

The Apprentice

My final task on *The Apprentice*—the ultimate challenge that would decide the winner—was to put on a charity polo event. I had no control over my team, because they had already been fired. They had nothing to work for but their own self-respect, and I certainly counted on that in the selection process. I picked Elizabeth first, because she was a strong marketer, and John second, because he was a real workhorse and someone I liked. And finally I looked at Raj. He had made quite an impression on the show with his wardrobe and wandering eye. He was sitting there in his trademark bow tie. I said, "We're going to a polo field, Raj; you're perfect!"

I focused on appealing to my team members' duty. They had nothing to lose, I certainly understood that. So I told them right at the start, "I want to win this, and I'd appreciate your support. I know you want to do well coming back in the final episode to show the world that you shouldn't have been fired." All three of them really came through.

The polo match was a great success. But in boardroom discussions with Donald, Carolyn, and George, I got an earful for not having Mr. Trump's seat cleaned at the polo field. I said: "That was my fault, Mr. Trump, everyone was kicking butt, doing everything I asked, and that was one of the details I planned to take care of. I accept full responsibility. It was not appropriate—I should have taken more care to have the VIP area all set up, and I didn't do it." And that was that. Taking responsibility ended the conversation.

This wasn't a gimmick or a trick. Ultimately, it was my fault. I didn't oversee somebody to see that the seat was cleaned. There was no reason to point the finger at Elizabeth or Raj or John and say they should have taken care of it. Elizabeth was doing a fantastic job setting up a great dinner and live auction with entertainment by Tony Bennett after the polo game. John and Raj were doing their parts too. Another problem had come up with the sign for one of our sponsors—it was blown over by the wind and got broken. This fell into Elizabeth's area, and she had informed me that the sign wasn't up, but I made the decision from a priority standpoint that we needed to finish sorting out the dinner arrangements.

Now in the boardroom Carolyn and George kept saying, "The sponsor is really upset, nothing was set up...wasn't that Elizabeth's area?" Almost trying to get me to point the finger and say, yes, she should have done that. What I said was "It was my fault. She notified me that the sign wasn't fixed. She had maxed out her resources of what she was capable of doing and it was back in my queue. I didn't reassign it or take care of it myself, so it was my fault."

Again, because I took responsibility, that discussion ended. In the military I was taught not to take all the credit and assign all the blame. Duty means taking responsibility for everything. Whatever went wrong was my fault, because I needed to manage the team better so they could finish their tasks. Or I could do them myself. I certainly wasn't going to say: "Oh we had a great event, a big success, I did it all...and those two little things that got screwed up? That was Elizabeth." My team had done a great job for me and I wanted to make that clear to the Trump people and to everyone watching the show. My team had done its best. It was my job as leader to take responsibility for making sure everything was done right—down to the very last detail.

years of service ahead. I never even had a thought of leaving the Academy early.

"Four years, when you're a young kid, seems like an eternity. But I knew exactly what the deal was: four years of school, and a four-year Navy obligation. I certainly had the desire and the ability to play professional football. But I really enjoyed the camaraderie at the Naval Academy and in the military. I absolutely wanted to do my duty. When I graduated I wasn't sure I would ever play football again, and I was all right with that. If I hadn't played pro football, there's a good chance I would have stayed in the Navy as a career."

An equally compelling example of someone with an incredible sense of duty is the late Pat Tillman. He was a man who had it all: PAC-10 defensive player of the year at Arizona State University, a fantastic player for the Arizona Cardinals, he was living at a level that maybe one-tenth of one percent of the entire population is capable of reaching. But after 9/11, when the call went out that the U.S needed Special Forces troops, he volunteered to do his duty. He turned down a $3 million-plus contact with the Cardinals to enlist in the Army, undergo Ranger training, and ship out to Afghanistan. Pat Tillman fought for a cause he believed was just and paid the ultimate price. No one ever said that doing your duty is easy, or comes without great cost.

Doing your duty means taking orders—sometimes from people you disagree with. You might not agree with your company's direction or your boss's latest decision, but doing your duty as an employee or team member means no bellyaching. Get with your team, get with the program, and do your part to accomplish the mission. Your day-to-day responsibilities and obligations at work—all the tasks you are charged with in whatever role you fill at your organization—none of these should be things that require constant monitoring or lots of discussion. Just do it.

Duty goes beyond executing orders, it means assessing and doing what needs to be done. It means asking, "What's the overall mission for my job, and my employee's job, in this company?" This thinking is straight from the military. Military personnel take to heart the idea of "How do I make sure that the overall mission is accomplished?"

The military and almost every business operate in team environments. A good commander in the military wants to hear input from all his soldiers, because the ramification of low morale and poor performance are death. It is much easier to fall in line and "do your duty" in the military, because you have been trained that way. You take a direct order and follow what your officer says, period. It's second nature, something that has been ingrained from the moment you signed up. It makes for efficiency and effectiveness. Just before a decision is made and an order given, an officer reflects on training, doctrine, strategy, circumstances, resources, and personnel. No military decision is ever made willy-nilly.

Duty does not mean blind obedience. A soldier can actually be prosecuted for following an unlawful order, as in the movie *A Few Good Men*. In the private sector, the same principle applies. You might have to execute orders you don't like, but there is no excuse for dishonesty, immorality, or illegality. Behaving honorably is your most important duty to yourself and your organization. You can't plead ignorance. You can't say, "I was just doing what my boss told me to do!" As the boss, you can't whine, "I was just following the plan my CFO or accountant laid out." You must follow your internal moral compass. As a leader, especially a CEO or a board member, you have a duty to protect shareholder's interests. And as an employee, it might sometimes become your unfortunate duty to speak up when you identify underhanded or shady behavior.

> Management is doing things right; leadership is doing the right things.
>
> —PETER DRUCKER

Pete Dawkins is currently vice chairman of The Citigroup Private Bank, providing sophisticated wealth management services to clients worldwide. An outstanding cadet and athlete at West Point, and a distinguished military leader who retired as a brigadier general, he has been a student of leadership for many years. He told me, "One of the tyrannies of large organizations is that it often doesn't matter how good the overall organization is. If your immediate boss is a loser, your world is at best frustrating, and potentially a dead end." On another note, he observed that, "In formal organizations it's a tough call to tell the boss something he doesn't want to hear. There's a lot of talk about 'speaking up,' yet most people know when you tell the boss that what he is proposing is wrong, there's a good chance you won't change his mind. Furthermore, you may get fired or, more likely, find—years later—that doing so disadvantaged you down the line. The fact is, it takes courage to speak up, and it's risky. It's a very personal choice. It really comes down to, 'How do we want to live our lives?'"

As a leader your obligations are greater, and your standards must be even higher. Let's take a very small, simple example: say you work at a company with its main office in a large suburban office park. A bunch of employees are returning from their lunch break and see some trash scattered on the lawn of corporate headquarters. Most of them won't even give it a second glance. They barely even see it, and they certainly don't feel any need to pick it up. They just aren't invested enough, or feel a large enough sense of duty to the company. But if someone who owns shares in the company walks by? A board member, the CEO, the president? You want employees who will pick up the trash, who will do their duty, in the big picture and down to the smallest detail. And someone who's served in the military? Not only will they pick up the trash, they'll make sure no one litters, to boot.

At the time I applied for *The Apprentice*, I had been out of the Army for ten years and had a number of entrepreneurial ventures behind me. When I was told I had been chosen for the show, I was a businessman living in San Diego. I had pressing obligations to two businesses. I was president of CoreObjects, a software development company, where over three years the role had evolved from part-time consultant, to a half-time employee responsible for corporate development, to full-time president. At the same time I was consumed with growing MotorPride, a website for car enthusiasts, the first business I had conceived and built from the ground up with my friend and business partner Jon Kraft.

> The buck stops here.
>
> —HARRY S. TRUMAN

I talked to my business partners about my new commitment. During the filming of the show, I would be totally out-of-pocket. No calling in every day, checking messages, or following up with the clients. And, of course, in the event I won, I would be completely removed from the businesses for at least one year and maybe forever.

Because of the strong team we had developed over three years at CoreObjects, I wasn't uncomfortable about leaving. One of the greatest accomplishments during my time there was building such a great team. I had every confidence in them, and did not worry about "going missing" for an extended period.

MotorPride, however, was in a completely different position. It would be a great deal of slack for my partner, Jon Kraft, to pick up.

Luckily we had grown to the point where it was the right time to bring on a general manager. So we hired Klaus Holzapfel, a great marketer with a special interest in cars. We had the business model down and now we had the manager to make it work. In retrospect, we had to wonder why we didn't do this sooner. Note to self and all of you entrepreneurs out there: Hire experts with deep "domain knowledge" to manage your businesses as soon as possible! In the Army, that's why we have warrant officers.

I felt I could leave both CoreObjects and MotorPride because we had built them the right way with the right people: It is a hallmark of a good organization that it inspires people to grow and learn. Many of these people will eventually want to leave for new challenges. A good organization understands and even welcomes this.

In the military, assignments are being changed all the time, and units learn to adapt; the military knows that duty includes doing the right thing for its people and developing their skills, even if it means moving that individual to another unit. In the private sector, a perfect example is McKinsey Consulting. When an employee says he wants to pursue other opportunities, McKinsey's response is: "Great, you'll continue to be paid for as long as you need to be (within reason). Do you need an office for a while? How about a secretary to help?" McKinsey understands that an ambitious person going to another business might become a client some day—or rejoin the company with new skills and experience.

That whole defensive short-term perspective of "You can't leave!" or "Pack up your stuff and get out right now!" is simply bad management, bad business, and bad leadership. The military actually makes a point of cross-training people, assigning them to ports around the country and around the world, of sending people to school. Officers understand that it's not a matter of loss to unit, but of ultimate gain for the Army. Likewise at CoreObjects, we make a point of congratulating departing valued employees, letting them know how much we'd like them back, and how much we'd love to do business with their new company.

When I won my spot on *The Apprentice*, this same congratulatory response was given to me, and I was grateful for it. We made sure my responsibilities were covered; we thought of how I could leverage my opportunity for the benefit of our companies; and we talked about what sort of useful exposure our companies could get.

When I became Donald Trump's Apprentice, I recognized a new duty: to represent my former companies and colleagues as best as I could—and that included my brothers (literally, in the case of three of my four younger brothers) and sisters in the military. Did serving in the military help me win *The Apprentice*? I know it helped me— and instilling in me a devotion to duty was a big part of it.

• • •

Jim Kimsey on Duty

Jim Kimsey is a West Point graduate, member of the Ranger Hall of Fame, founder of AOL and noted philanthropist. During our meeting he reminisced about his days as a cadet:

> I attended West Point in the late fifties/early sixties, a time when the Academy was kind of idealized. The long gray line...there was a television program called "West Point" airing each week

back then, and every kid in America wanted to go there. Those guys were famous. Quite frankly, I figured at the time if I went to West Point I'd probably do very well with the ladies. I didn't count on them never letting us out!

I was not what could be called a great cadet. It was a tremendously restrictive environment, particularly back in those days, and I can't say I liked that too much. In retrospect I must credit West Point with a great deal, up to and including keeping me out of jail. I remember the very first day I arrived for the beginning of Beast Barracks, which was quite an in-your-face shock. I was told there were only three answers to every question: "YES, SIR," "NO, SIR" and "NO EXCUSE, SIR." It took me a long time to fully appreciate and internalize what that really meant. Internalizing and living by the idea that there was NO EXCUSE was a very valuable lesson I've carried throughout my life. It means that you bear responsibility for all of your own actions, and as a leader you bear responsibility for the welfare of those in your organization and the outcome of its missions.

If you lead men into combat and some of your men get killed, that's going to be you personally explaining to a mother why their kid died. There's no excuse for that. And if you're CEO of a large organization and have to lay off 3000 people, there's no excuse for that either. I believe that once you internalize the idea that you bear full responsibility for your actions, it pushes you to think ahead far enough to ensure that whatever you undertake will have a successful outcome. Because the bottom line is that there is no excuse for not having a success-ful outcome.

People who deal with me realize that explanations are one thing, but I try to lead my life in a "no excuses" way, and expect that others will follow my example. Which is why I like to hire employees who attended West Point or are military vet-erans of any branch. I know that among their many other valu-able skills, they have most certainly learned the lesson of accountability and will bring it to bear for the good of my orga-nization.

TAKE COMMAND: DUTY

You know what to do 99 percent of the time. When an employee asks me a question, I look him in the eye and ask, "What's the right thing to do?" Almost every time he can make the decision on his own. So stop waiting for someone to tell you what to do. Be active and do the right thing. This applies to both your work and your personal life. "Just Do It!"

CHAPTER TWO

Impeccability: If Something Is Worth Doing, Then It's Worth Doing Right

As the Apprentice, I have observed Donald Trump deal with a dizzying number of partners, vendors, and subcontractors on his many different ventures. To work with the Trump Organization, a company has to be impeccable. Its credentials and reputation must be spotless, and woe to anyone who hasn't done his research before presenting a business plan or budget to Donald. The bar for quality is set sky-high in terms of his brand, which is the reason he has been able to create so much value in his organization. A Trump property is clean, neat, well-constructed, high-quality, and loaded with every possible amenity. A customer looking to buy a condominium or rent office space for their headquarters has a level of assurance the moment they consider a Trump property. Any building—whether it's a towering office skyscraper in midtown Manhattan or condos in Florida—increases in value anywhere from 50 to 80 percent once the Trump logo is attached and Donald becomes involved. That's the power of the brand he's created, and the expectation of impeccability.

Impeccability means free from fault or blame; flawless. And a big part of impeccability means attention to detail. Attention to detail is critical in war. It means knowing how many rounds each solider has left for his weapon, how much weight he has in his pack, and the precise distance and location of where he needs to march. Everything in the military has to be exact. If you're a soldier calling in artillery fire, you'd better be providing accurate coordinates for the enemy six hundred yards away from your location. You can't argue with exploding artillery rounds or say "Whoops, I was off a little." The consequences for a lack of attention to detail are severe—physical injury and death.

> Get the facts, or the facts will get you. And when you get them, get them right, or they will get you wrong.
>
> —DR. THOMAS FULLER

Teaching an attention to detail is the force behind many of the seemingly incomprehensible activities at West Point. As plebes, we were required to read and memorize the front page and the sports page of the *New York Times* every single day before breakfast formation. Upperclassmen quizzed us on the contents of the newspaper throughout the day. We were also charged to memorize a vast array of military information—the missions of the various branches of the service, specifications of weapon systems, and anniversaries of historic battles.

Because we were drilled mercilessly by upperclassmen every day, we had to become adept at absorbing, memorizing, and being able to convey lots of information under intense pressure, quickly and accurately.

I'd be standing in place in my company formation and an upperclassman would yell out, "Hey, Perdew, how did the Red Sox do this week?" If I didn't know the answer, they would come over and get in my face until I responded appropriately. If I couldn't come up with a satisfactory answer, I could be reprimanded. The more times I missed an answer, the more attention I drew to myself. This could snowball significantly until I found myself spending that evening after dinner reporting to upperclassmen's rooms with correct answers and wasting my very precious time. At West Point, time was so very, very important because you had so little of it at your disposal.

Plebes also had to memorize all three of the meals for the day, and who the officer in charge was for that day. Some cadets were charged with delivering all the mail; others delivered all the laundry. Some plebes called out the minutes before formations so that upperclassmen would know when to be ready and what to wear. Everyone had a task, believe me. Think about this for a minute, if you will: every day, four thousand cadets ate breakfast in fifteen to twenty minutes. Each table had two or three plebes at the end to serve all of the upperclassmen. And as plebes, we had to know each upperclassman's preferences—from what kind of food they preferred to the number of ice cubes they wanted in their iced tea—which might vary from the number of ice cubes they wanted in their Coke.

If there was a dessert at dinner that required cutting, such as cake or pie, we were required to cut it into identically sized pieces, using up the entire pie. You try to do that when only seven people want pie! Seven pieces, exactly the same size, with no crumbs left on the top of the cake and none left in the pan. By the way, for cakes with icing, using a protractor and a cold iced knife is the best way to do it. I know from experience. It was high art for a plebe.

Varsity athletes at West Point sat at "corps squad" tables, which was preferential seating if you will, so they didn't have undue stress during meals. They were also allowed to eat as much as they wanted so they could compete effectively on the playing field. But for the rest of us plebes, at meals we sat straight up, the table a fist's distance from our stomach and the chair back a fist's distance from our spine. Our eyes stayed fixed on the crests on our plates. When we took a bite, it did not exceed the size of anything that would require us to chew more than two times and swallow after we were addressed. We had to respond without food in our mouths. Under these constraints, it was usually pretty hard to get a full meal in!

> An expert is a man who has made all the mistakes which can be made in a very narrow field.
>
> —NIELS BOHR

Everything about our days included massive memorization of minutiae and attention to the tiniest details. Much of it seemed crazy at the time, but the training would serve us well as soldiers.

After I graduated from West Point, I completed my Military Intelligence Officer Basic Course and earned my Ranger Tab, which I'll discuss in more detail later. I then reported to my first unit—2nd Brigade, 7th Infantry Division (Light) at Ford Ord, California. I was the assistant intelligence (S-2) officer for an infantry brigade of 1,500 soldiers. A brigade is the primary fighting force unit, which is further broken down into battalions, then companies and finally platoons and squads. There were three brigades in the 7th Infantry Division, and each brigade rotated through monthly turns serving on a 2-hour recall as a rapid deployment force. That meant that every soldier on call had to be standing in formation ready to move out within two hours of an alert going out. As an infantry brigade we had support from field artillery, military intelligence, air defense artillery, and other supporting elements. As a light infantry brigade, we were basically troops on foot, without armor protection, though we did have Humvees.

As the assistant S-2, I was responsible for supporting the S-2 and filling in for him when he was gone. I worked with then Captain Andrew Hergenrother, who later appeared on *The Apprentice* to say some very nice things about me to Donald Trump. I was humbled to hear his remarks, because this man had amazing attention to detail plus incredible passion for his job. Captain Hergenrother was a great leader. He embodied the Army's principles of leadership. He had been an enlisted soldier before completing Officer Candidate School, so he had significant experience in the military at every level.

> Skill comes from practice.
>
> —CHINESE PROVERB

Every one of the ten principles I discuss in this book was second nature to him. He honed them every day, and hammered them into me and the other soldiers as we worked together.

The brigade commander was Colonel Linwood E. Burney, who was the ranking surviving officer from Hamburger Hill in Vietnam. He impressed upon me, the entire brigade, and pretty much everyone he ever came in contact with that soldiering was not "just a job." We were not training merely to learn how to shoot things. We were going into combat together, where all of us would depend on each other. Anybody who screwed up or didn't carry their weight would seriously jeopardize soldiers' lives. Colonel Burney was very serious about our mission of being ready to go to war. We've all heard the saying, "You don't get a second chance to make a first impression." In combat, a bad "first impression" equals death. I never met another soldier who had quite that level of intensity and focus; he was an awesome and inspiring motivator. In turn, his soldiers got things done for him.

The level of intensity was maintained at all times during our training program. Everything we did, we were doing for a serious reason. No fun and games, lollygagging, or daydreaming about an upcoming three-day pass. Our mindset was: We are professional soldiers, and we are going to war. We *must* be ready. Once we're in a war, it's too late to train and try to figure out what's going on. All of our training exercises met Colonel Burney's exacting standards of impeccability. He tolerated nothing less. And because of that, if you'd asked any soldier who they'd want commanding them in combat, the answer was always Colonel Burney.

After I left the Army, I entered UCLA Law School with the intent of becoming a corporate attorney. At West Point I had completed a summer internship with the House Armed Services Committee in Washington, D.C. Because of my top-secret security clearance, I was able to sit in on the mark-up hearings of bills and see how laws in this country are really made. This experience certainly planted the seed for my later interest in both business and the law. I realized how true Calvin Coolidge's famous phrase really is: that the business of America is business. Every legislative decision had to do with jobs, allocating tax dollars (generated by the private sector), keeping our economy competitive, and allocating contracts for government business.

I researched how to become an effective corporate attorney. Every attorney I talked to said a strong background in business was a big plus—it was the one trait most often lacking in candidates for corporate law firms. I decided that as I studied for my law degree, I would earn an MBA at UCLA's Anderson Business School simultaneously. During my JD/MBA program, the first year I only took law classes. The second year I attended the business school, but loaded a couple of law school classes onto my workload. At the same time I got a job working twenty hours a week at Gibson, Dunn & Crutcher, a prominent national law firm. I worked for Gibson during my second and third years of school. My third and fourth years of study I combined both law and business classes, graduating with degrees in both at the end of four years.

I've been told a few times in my life that I like to argue, and the study of law was a great place to practice my arguments. There is nothing like having a law school professor rip your carefully prepared argument to shreds. Law school taught me the importance of impeccable research. If you aren't diligent and perfect in your research when preparing a case, rest assured that opposing counsel will be. If as a lawyer, you fail to study and commit to memory every last precedent and legal decision with any application to your client's case, you will suffer the ramifications in court, in front of the judge. Your client's money, business—or, in criminal cases, freedom—depends in large part upon your attention to detail and impeccable research.

The whole business versus law debate came to a head one day during my third year of law school. In the course of my twenty-hour workweek at Gibson, Dunn & Crutcher, I labored for months on the corporate acquisition of a company worth tens of millions of dollars. My law firm represented the corporation acquiring the smaller company. When it was finally time to close the deal, a bunch of us had been up all night at the printer finalizing the documents for the purchase agreement. The room was packed with lawyers and accountants and principals from both sides. At 10:00 a.m. we were all bleary with bloodshot eyes when the owner of the smaller company strolled in with his CFO. They were both big guys, from Texas, wearing cowboy hats and boots and smoking cigars.

> Some gentleman says I have been a tailor. That does not disconcert me in the least; for when I was a tailor I had the reputation of being a good one, and making close fits; I was always punctual with my customers, and always did good work.
>
> —PRESIDENT ANDREW JOHNSON

The two men took seats at the long wooden table, where a partner from Gibson, Dunn & Crutcher was arguing with the acquiring company's lead attorney. The issue was where a comma should be placed in one of the contract's clauses. The CFO turned to the CEO and said, "Can you believe we're paying these sons-of-bitches $500 an hour to argue about where a comma goes?"

I looked at both of the attorneys at the end of the table. Both were highly regarded partners in their respective top-drawer law firms— extremely capable and bright. Both had contributed immeasurably to getting this deal done. But at the moment, they were arguing about a comma. I looked over at the guy in boots smoking a cigar about to make millions on one deal, and the light bulb went on: *I wanted to be the client.* I wanted to be the person creating companies and building wealth. Everything had suddenly become crystal clear: I didn't want to be a vendor, or a consultant, or an attorney. I wanted to be the guy running the companies and hiring the lawyers.

I was meeting so many talented people at Anderson Business School who were jumping into the business world and starting all kinds of exciting ventures. My entrepreneurial passion grew and grew until in my final year, when I wrote a business plan for ImageTel, a videoconferencing start-up company. My law classes gave me an excellent grounding in learning how laws govern and drive our society; it was a strong underpinning to the rest of my education. And I have used what I learned in law school significantly, in terms of regulations, the ins and outs of setting up corporations, and simply understanding the fundamental notion that much of business rests on contracts. My law degree has been tremendously useful in my career, but my heart was in business—specifically, in starting and growing companies.

Another great story about impeccability is how the company eteamz grew to be the largest amateur sports portal in existence. The eteamz founders, Brian Johnson and Aaron Eisenberg, were twenty-something friends who lived in southern California. Brian got disenchanted with law school at Berkeley, dropped out in the middle of his first year and returned home. The only thing he knew he wated to do (besides burn his resume) was coach a Little League baseball team...so he volunteered. Unfortunately, although a good athlete in his playing days, Brian's team looked like the Bad News Bears, and the kids' morale dropped with every loss.

Brian wanted these kids to have a better experience. He thought there should be a way for talented, passionate, successful coaches to share their knowledge with volunteer coaches and kids. That started Brian thinking: What can we do to provide that information? He collaborated with his friend Aaron, an internet developer, and together they created a system to track schedules, standings, rosters, directions to the game, even who was in charge of cookies that week for various leagues and teams. A separate section of the website was designed to make available tips, drills, and instructions in any sport. Anyone who became coach of a tee-ball team could go to their website and get direction on everything from lists of necessary equipment to how to set up a practice.

Brian reached out to webmasters trying to develop websites for their sports teams. He asked them every question he could think of. What's the hardest thing about coaching your team? What information is most important for your website? What would you like to see done better? What information would most help your team? What information would most help the kids' parents? Brian and Aaron did an unbelievably thorough job of product assessment—talking with future customers about what the product should be. From those hundreds of discussions with coaches and parents, they created their product: a website called eteamz. Pretty soon they had about seven hundred or eight hundred baseball teams using their site, and contributing tips and drills. It was mostly about baseball to start, though it was clear that this was a model that could easily be applied to every amateur sport across the board—football, bowling, horseshoes, you name it.

Gary Weinhouse, who served as eteamz's VP of operations, was also attending the Anderson Business School at UCLA. He suggested putting the eteamz business plan into the business school's annual competition. The eteamz concept won. I learned about the project through my business school alumni network and was immediately drawn in. At this point I had been through one failed entrepreneurial venture and been hard at work at Deloitte Consulting for two years in a regular salaried job trying to recover from my financial losses at ImageTel. I was eager to get back into the entrepreneurial start-up mode, and the eteamz idea and team got me fired up enough to leave my so-called "secure" position at Deloitte Consulting.

Eteamz was a perfect combination of so many things I personally am passionate about: team sports, kids, and growing a business. The challenge was turning this great idea into a profitable company. This was at the height of the Internet craze, so we focused on trying to capture all the "eyeballs" we could on our site, create loyalty, and worry about profits later. In the Internet boom days, that was the plan. Very few people anticipated that the bubble would burst and the money faucet would be shut off.

We recruited Anderson graduates and interns from the summer program to work with us at eteamz. We did a great job of the entrepreneurial basics: networking and utilizing our resources.

After we won the business plan competition, we were able to attract $1 million from the Tech Coast Angels, an investment group that specializes in start-up technology companies. That capital allowed us to make critical hires including experts in various sports so that we could provide credible content in each of our most popular sports communities. We spent the next year acquiring online companies who had traction in various sports, with the goal of getting plenty of expertise in-house. There might be a guy in Iowa who had the best website on being an offensive lineman on a football team. We'd give him an eteamz hat and a set of business cards and say, "You don't have to worry about the technology anymore. Come be our expert on offensive line drills, tips, and instruction on eteamz. Your name will be up in lights and there's no more technology hassle."

Users could go on the site and see little Johnny smiling as he ran into home plate, and we provided a guest book where Aunt Edna in Ohio could post, "Great job, Johnny, sorry we couldn't be at the

---

The Apprentice

My favorite task on *The Apprentice* was the Pepsi Challenge, where our team had to create a new bottled drink for the Pepsi-Cola company. I was project manager and got to send one person to the other team. I sent Jen to the other team with Andy and Sandy, which worked out very well. Ivana, Kevin, and I were a well-oiled machine. We set up a plan on the way to Pepsi's headquarters and got that spreadsheet rocking. We had all of our meetings set up by the time we arrived. We walked through the creative process and together came up with what we believed was a fantastic bottle design. It was the word "EDGE" turned sideways. "Check the Box, Get the Edge! " was our motto, so we wanted a bottle with an actual hole that went all the way through the letter D in EDGE. Inside the hole, we could put sweepstakes tickets and other prizes and use it as a promotional tool. However, we kept getting told by the engineers that a bottle with a hole would be too difficult to make and mass-produce. We stuck to our guns, because it was the perfect bottle, and we weren't about to settle for anything less than perfection. Yes, it was hard to do, but we pushed them and we got it done. That bottle won the day. It looked great. We insisted on—and won with—an impeccable product design.

game!" The networking effect was simply phenomenal. For example, we had twelve-year old girls' soccer teams in Europe all signing each others' guest books, teams from Germany, France, and England. The girls actually set up a summer tour based on their communication on eteamz, traveling to play each other. Eteamz changed the amateur sports world. It allowed people to focus on what they loved doing—the sports—instead of the worrying about organization, technology, and communication.

Because of Brian's focus on an impeccable product, in less than two years, eteamz became the third-most trafficked sports website. After a year, eteamz had fifty thousand softball tournaments listed on the site. The only two sports websites that showed more traffic than eteamz were CBS Sportsline and ESPN. We had more traffic than the PGA Tour and NASCAR!

It is easy to see why we grew the way we did. There are usually ten to twenty kids on a Little League team, and most of them play more than one sport. They had brothers and sisters who play other sports and mom and dad might be in a bowling league. We created so many mechanisms to fuel growth that today, as this book goes to press, there are more than 2.5 million teams using the eteamz website, which encompasses every sport in every country in the world.

After raising the original million dollars, we raised approximately $4 million more from venture capitalists, for further expansion. We had a twenty-three-year-old and a twenty-five-year-old as founders, and only one person in the company was over forty. We were able to recruit the man who had grown adidas to a $1.6 billion dollar brand. He eventually became my first true business mentor—Steve Wynne, a phenomenal businessman.

I learned about unbelievable passion and impeccability from Brian, who was almost ten years younger than I was and with no formal business background. His dedication to customer satisfaction was absolute and inspiring. Those qualities came through so strongly in the product that eteamz was thought of by its users as an almost religious experience. Our customer service goal was to make sure that anyone who came to the website could find anything they needed instantly. If they were left with a question, we answered it—and fixed it—immediately. Brian was fond of asking, "When we have a million teams, what if each team asks one question?" The answer was, we'd be out of business, so we worked to ensure that the website was laid out correctly right from the start. And it was. The whole idea was to make an impeccable product—and that's why eteamz succeeded.

Eteamz had two main competitors: Myteam out of Boston and Active.com out of San Diego. What was ironic was that Myteam actually had the official sponsorship of Little League. Myteam had approached the Little League organization and offered to pay to be their official provider of this type of service. But eteamz, founded on offering a product that offered the user a great experience, focused on capturing new teams by outstanding word-of-mouth recommendations. With a little more than $5 million in funding we were killing Myteam on sports team adoption—especially inside of Little League! As it turned out, in Little League, as in many large organizations, regional volunteers didn't care much for headquarters. Little League teams around the country wanted the best product, and we had it, so they used it. And we constantly adjusted the product on a weekly and monthly basis to provide everything our users wanted.

Our other big competitor was Active.com. Active.com had orig-inally provided support for running events. If you wanted to regis-ter for a marathon, Active was the site for you. The people who actually managed the Boston Marathon, for example, used Active.com as their administrative tool for everything from online registration to marketing, to pricing, to scheduling.

As a customer or marathon runner or triathlete, I would come to their site to connect to local hotels, pay my admission fee, get my registration papers mailed to my house, and take care of many other details. It streamlined the entire process and was a great tool, but Active.com was eager to grow from individual events—like marathons and triathlons—into team sports.

Similarly, during eteamz's first year, we focused mainly on Little League baseball, but we soon targeted the next most popular sports: soccer, football, and others. We wanted to follow the kids from sport to sport, to keep our traffic up all year round. So we brought on pro-fessional athletes to help us market ourselves to different team sports. And we lived what we worked. Sometimes we'd play pickup basketball after meetings. It was ferociously competitive. Active had very much the same culture, employing triathletes and Ironman com-petitors. To build a successful product you have to hire the sort of people who would use it, who would know what it should be, and how it could be improved. Brian did that research at the beginning, but fine-tuning a product to achieve maximum customer satisfaction is a continual process.

We had gone about our business thinking that money would always be available from fundraising, and focused mainly on blow-ing out the product. There were a couple of revenue generators for eteamz. In order to host a website and have your team listed, it was free up to a certain point, based on how much space you took up. With lots of photos, adding video, or utilizing our fundraising tools, packages could be bought for a minimal amount of money per month. To host a website—or have a premium version—required a modest fee.

Advertisers—the Gatorades and Wilsons of the world—were another way to generate revenue. The amateur sporting goods market is a $4 billion dollar a year industry, and what better place to advertise than eteamz? Brian and I bumped heads frequently about when and how best to charge the users and bring in more advertisers. Brian wanted to protect the user experience. He worried that teams wouldn't want to share space with Gatorade ads. I wanted to generate income as quickly as possible, and argued that if part of our service was to keep the site free of ads, then he should charge for it—kind of like an HBO. But eteamz was a labor of love for Brian and we stayed true to his instinct. The creative tension between us contributed to sharpening the product and making eteamz a success.

> I find that the harder I work, the more luck I seem to have.
>
> —THOMAS JEFFERSON

When the Internet market imploded, Myteam and Active.com had each raised thirty to fifty million dollars. We lacked that huge war chest and were not on the same page as our investors about how to proceed. Ultimately, we decided to cut our reliance on investment capital and instead raise money from the site by shifting our traffic to a site that would become the de facto leader in amateur sporting sites.

We decided that our best bet, after a lengthy decision-making process, was to pare down from fifty people to a minimum number of employees—ten or twelve—so that we could still manage operations and continue to show growth month-to-month in our traffic. We terminated almost forty people over a three-month period and still continued to sustain our traffic growth rate, even without those employees.

At that point we were then able to approach both Myteam and Active.com and say, "All right, time to bid." We engaged an investment bank to help us in the auction of the company, and finally decided that Active.com was the buyer for the business. We had fifty thousand tournaments on our site, and between two to three hundred thousand teams. Our traffic was off the charts. Active.com's ability to take the entire package, do sponsorships, complete transactions, and maintain and develop the drills and tips sections combined into a phenomenally "feel good" business.

We wound up selling eteamz to Active.com for a little more than two-and-a-half times our invested capital. Keep in mind, this was after the Internet bubble burst, when most Internet companies were getting bought for pennies on the dollar, if at all, and at that time we were a company with no revenue. But Steve Wynne's insight and planning, along with the proven product and loyal customer base, paid off.

Active.com grew rapidly through acquisitions, and suddenly, there were a lot of chiefs—all the CEOs from the companies they had acquired. I negotiated a cash bonus for myself to get the sale done, retained a bit of equity, and went on my way. Active.com bought what was left of Myteam a few months later.

Brian stayed on at Active.com for six months, but finally decided he wanted to build another business. He is now in the middle of another labor of love called Zaadz. He wants to be able to provide every "mom and pop" storefront owner with an easy site-building tool that includes built-in, comprehensive marketing, commerce, and how-to-run-a-business components. He's focused on the personal improvement sector, and is looking to do for yoga studios, career coaches, and karate dojos what he did for Little League teams. He wants to reach people who don't have the time or knowledge to develop top-flight business websites. It's another phenomenal idea and service. Brian is a visionary.

There are two types of entrepreneurs. The first is an industry veteran who sees a problem and goes out to fix it with a new product or service that fixes that problem, and become the expert on that area. They can build the product or service. The other kind of an entrepreneur is the expert at growing a new company, which is what I like to do. I have been a marketing expert, a finance expert, a business developer, a CEO, a COO, and a board member. Through networking, I know how to find the experts every new company needs. (Tip: LinkedIn is an online tool that helps me stay in touch or find the right person in my vast network.)

Brian was the first kind of entrepreneur. The man recognized a market need. His passion was a critical aspect of eteamz's success, and the standard of impeccability he insisted on made the business work. Active.com is still going strong, with some of eteamz's original employees. When I check out the website (*www.eteamz.com*), and I see how it's grown to encompass sports I've never heard of, it simply amazes me and I tip my hat to Brian's genius.

You can't teach genius, but you can teach impeccability. In the military, officers are taught the necessity of gathering information to make an informed decision, knowing that it's impossible to gather 100 percent of the information you need. On the battlefield or in business, you have to make decisions with imperfect information all the time. Timing is critical, and every leader must decide when the research ends and the product is launched. Neither a combat leader nor an entrepreneur can afford indecision. One of the skills that sets Donald Trump apart is his ability to make decisions and forge ahead. He's a master at coming up with the right answer from imperfect information.

• • •

Ross Perot on Impeccability

Ross Perot was an outstanding cadet and naval officer in the 1950s and eventually became one of our country's most successful entrepreneurs:

> In high school I focused on working and learning to be a businessman. I was not preoccupied with being an honor student, even though all of my friends were. A turning point in my life occurred one day in high school when a great English teacher named Mrs. Duck asked me to stay after class. She looked me squarely in the eye and said, "Ross, why aren't you smart like all your friends?"
>
> My response was, "Mrs. Duck, I am as smart as they are, but they study all the time. I have other interests."

She replied, "Ross, talk is cheap. If you are as smart as they are, let me see some results." I took the challenge and studied hard night and day from that point on. On my next report card, I had all A's but one. For the rest of my time in high school, I got excellent grades. Mrs. Duck gave me the incentive to create an academic record that would allow me an appointment to the U.S. Naval Academy. She changed my life. A few years later, at the end of my freshman year at the Academy, I had gotten excellent grades in English. I felt a strong obligation to thank Mrs. Duck, so when I arrived home in Texarkana for the summer I went to her home and personally thanked her.

She expressed genuine surprise that I had done so well in English. This was very consistent with her usual way of motivating me. She then said, "Ross, why didn't you just write me a letter?"

I replied, "Mrs. Duck, every paper I ever turned in to you came back circled with red notes about how I could make it better. I knew I could not write a letter with no mistakes in it, so I thought I would be better off personally thanking you."

Without laughing or even smiling, she said, "Ross, you are probably right." She kept the pressure on. I owe her a debt I can never repay.

TAKE COMMAND: IMPECCABILITY

Make sure the first—and last—impression you make is your best. Maintain impeccable standards for all your work, you never know who is going to see it or what it will be used for. What you deliver, and how you deliver it, is who you are. Be the best you can be.

CHAPTER THREE

Passion: Be Passionate About What You Do, and Do What You're Passionate About

Last year, a middle school teacher from upstate New York wrote to Norma Foederer, Donald Trump's long-time assistant at Trump Tower. He had incorporated *The Apprentice* into his lesson plans and told Norma what an impact the show had on his students, even including student letters to Mr. Trump detailing the lessons they'd learned.

The teacher and Norma stayed in touch. He wondered if Mr. Trump could speak to the class. A meeting was arranged for the next time his students had a field trip to New York City. The class assembled in Trump's restaurant at the bottom of Trump Tower. He spent a good half-hour with the students, talking, joking, and answering their questions.

One of the kids asked Donald what he liked to do for fun, outside of work, and his reply was: "I don't think I 'work' at all. I love what I'm doing so much that it is not work for me." Donald Trump only sleeps about four hours a night. He doesn't gamble, he doesn't do drugs, and he doesn't drink. He's married now, with a new baby on the way, so that will keep him a little busier at home!

But his overriding passion is to put real estate deals together. Just about the only other thing I could call him passionate about, outside of his work and his family, is the New York Yankees. Donald is good friends with George Steinbrenner, and Donald actually got to throw out the first pitch of a Yankees game, though it didn't go according to plan. But as always, Donald takes everything in stride.

Derek Jeter personally escorted Donald out to make the first pitch just in front of the pitcher's mound, and Donald got very impatient with the preliminaries. "Give me that ball!" he barked, then strode up to the rubber on the pitcher's mound. He wound up and threw to the catcher—and that ball hit the ground twice on the way to the plate. The whole crowd went crazy—they all started screaming as one, "You're fired!" Donald took it good-naturedly— even he had to smile at himself.

I knew exactly what Donald meant when he said work is not work, because that's just how I feel about building companies and my various new ventures at the Trump Organization. My passion in life is growing companies. People often look at me and scratch their heads, because when I'm in start-up company building mode I get so excited that I can't sleep. I wake up at 4 a.m. and start working on the computer. Next thing I know I look around and it's 2 p.m., I forgot to eat lunch, my hair's sticking straight up, and there I am in my boxer briefs calling overseas, faxing Los Angeles, trying to hammer out every last detail of a new deal.

When you really have passion for what you are doing, it impacts your success in so many different ways. Certainly the people who work for you feel it. The people you're working for will also feel it. You're happier, and everyone around you is happier. When you are not excited about what you're doing, it has equal impact, only in a negative manner. I've seen it in my own employees sometimes when they aren't excited about what they're doing; I've observed it in my own performance at times in my life when I was not enthused about where I was or the task at hand. Passion is an integral part of every one of Donald Trump's businesses, and a noticeable characteristic of every one of his employees. If you've ever seen George Ross or Carolyn Kepcher in action, you know what I'm talking about.

> One may have a blazing hearth in one's soul and yet no one ever came to sit by it. Passersby see only a wisp of smoke from the chimney and continue on their way.
>
> —VINCENT VAN GOGH

After finishing with my first start-up company (after the Army and law and business school), I found myself tapped out—physically and financially. So I called Deloitte Consulting. Deloitte had offered me a job earlier (I interned there when a student at Anderson Business School), and they put me to work immediately. Deloitte Consulting is the consulting arm of Deloitte & Touche, LLP, a very prominent accounting firm. Deloitte Consulting is a Big Five (or however many are left now) consulting firm with over five hundred employees in the Los Angeles office alone.

My job was working on teams to help technology companies. I helped develop an e-business plan for Motorola when they entered that market, and worked with Qwest on their strategy for their internet protocol backend. On each team I played a number of roles, from interviewing possible vendors to creating financial models predicting future market trends. You name it, I did it—and as an extra benefit I learned new skills and got to work with some incredibly talented team members.

But what I really liked doing was anticipating a company's challenges. I could spot them and say, "I can solve this for you and you guys need to be thinking about this, this, and this for your future."

Strategic forecasting that involved higher-end sales of services to meet new challenges was what I did best, and I was much happier in that role than as a researcher or financial modeler. But inside the Deloitte Consulting environment, just as in the military, every person had his specified role. With my entrepreneurial bent, I was bucking the trend a bit. I was a relatively junior person, but, like the more senior staff, I wanted a piece of the action. Deloitte Consulting did not offer sales incentives. I was an employee on a salary, so no matter how much business I sold to Motorola or Qwest, the check we got from them went to the partners and I was paid my base salary. But if I didn't have a personal stake in sales, I couldn't get passionate about the business. So after two years, I left Deloitte for a business I could be passionate about: eteamz.

I was in on the ground floor of several companies after I left Deloitte: eteamz, CoreObjects, and The Layoff Lounge. All these businesses taught me lessons, but I wanted to start one from an orig-

> It's the soul's duty to be loyal to its own desires. It must abandon itself to its master passion.
>
> —REBECCA WEST

inal idea—one of my own. I asked Jon Kraft, my old friend, to help me plan my next entrepreneurial venture. Jon was a very successful entrepreneur in his own right, and someone I had recruited to be the head of sales at CoreObjects, so we had a great working relationship. I was excited about working with him on a new venture, and he and I spent several weeks brainstorming.

In those days I occasionally commuted from San Diego to Los Angeles. While sitting in my car on the 405 freeway in bumper-to-bumper traffic, I looked around and asked myself, "How do I make a dollar off every one of these cars?" I noticed during all these endless hours on the freeway that every fifth or sixth car was a Honda Civic or an Acura Integra, and that the owner had clearly spent more money upgrading his vehicle than it had originally cost. Handles shaved off, windows tinted, dropped to the ground, fat tires, and shiny wheels...I realized how fanatical, proud, and obsessed with their vehicles so many people were. They lived to show them off.

At my previous company, eteamz, we had capitalized on the fact that people were proud of their kids and wanted to show off their athletic accomplishments. We helped customers showcase what their kids had done and provided great products to communicate with other teams, coaches, and players. If the model worked for sports, why not for car, truck, and motorcycle-enthusiasts?

In my initial research, I learned that there were countless varieties of car buffs, motorcycle buffs, and truck buffs in America. Low-riders, monster trucks, motocross—you name it. Every type of car, from old Model-Ts to muscle cars; from high-performance Porsches and Lamborghinis to putt-putt VW bugs, every make and model has a club and a devoted following in just about every city.

These motor vehicle fans spend a significant chunk of their disposable income refurbishing their cars, trucks, and motorcycles. It's called the automotive aftermarket, and it's a multi-billion-dollar-a-year industry driven by enthusiasts who love to hear that throaty deep sound when they turn the key in their high-performance Mustang. They live for the days they can take off on their classic Harleys and fly down the highway. Monster-truck fans can't wait for rallies and shows and spend every spare moment off-roading through the backwoods. I wanted to harness their passion with MotorPride, give these people a site that would serve their love of cars, trucks, and motorcycles, and help them share information with each other: everything from how to do personalized modifications to news about particular makes and models, bulletins about manufacturers' recalls and newly available accessories.

I discovered that most motor clubs had a lot of administrative headaches: from maintaining an accurate email list, to collecting dues, to broadcasting news about events and meetings. But with MotorPride, we could offer total administrative support. People could pay their dues online by credit card; they could register for events online; and they could buy club T-shirts, chat with other clubs nationwide, and post pictures from road trips. MotorPride could take care of everything and let motor enthusiasts get away from the computer and back behind the wheel.

Initially, Jon and I contacted more than three hundred automotive club owners. We asked what types of services they'd like to see in the MotorPride product. The most encouraging thing we learned was that nobody was currently providing them with the online services they needed.

We knew there was a place for MotorPride, so we set about building a team. I tapped a developer, a graphics person, and a back-end infrastructure wiring guy from eteamz. My business partner Jon put up some of the seed money so we could bootstrap the project ourselves and avoid all the "fun" aspects of raising money and managing investors. Through my network, I assembled a team that was prepared to execute.

In less than a year Jon and I had the MotorPride site up and running. And it was all done virtually. The developer, the network person, the graphics person, the user-interface person, none of these people ever met face-to-face. We did it all collaboratively, using technology and the eteamz model, with some specialized variations.

I should confess that although I love cars, I didn't know much about them. Starting MotorPride helped me learn so much more. And while I'm not an official car nut, I'm a company-building nut; I love being an entrepreneur and assembling a team to build something new. Teamwork is something the Army insists on—and just as a platoon officer leads his men everyday to accomplish a mission, I have brought that same drive, spirit, and training to assembling my own business platoon to create new products and services.

> We grow great by dreams. All big men are dreamers. They see things in the soft haze of a spring day or in the red fire of a long winter's evening. Some of us let these dreams die, but others nourish and protect them; nurse them through bad days till they bring them to the sunshine and light which comes always to those who hope that their dreams will come true.
>
> —WOODROW WILSON

Every platoon in the Army has men trained in a specialty. Similarly, my plan at MotorPride included bringing in experts to the site who could "speak" the same language as our users, anticipate their needs, and give the site credibility with people for whom Motor-Pride was more than the name of a website; it was a way of life. I needed someone to talk with the "Goodwrench" crowd. For every category, from Porsche to TransAms, we planned to have an expert to manage the forums and serve as the authority figure. The business began growing. And eventually, we were lucky to find Klaus, a passionate car nut, to serve as general manager while I competed on *The Apprentice*.

> The happiness of a man in this life does not consist in the absence but in the mastery of his passions.
>
> —ALFRED LORD TENNYSON

I always want my customers to have passion for my product—and that requires that the product be designed, marketed, and refined by people who share that passion.

A passionate attachment to impeccability and getting the job done is a military trait. It's a misconception that military people are robotic. If you want to see passion, check out the Army/Navy football game, one of the biggest sports rivalries there is. The esprit-de-corps, the feeling of belonging to something bigger than yourself, feeds passion. Yes, military training teaches you to control your emotions, but that's so you won't act like a fool under pressure. Rudyard Kipling describes the military ethos perfectly when he writes, "If you can keep your head when all those about you are losing theirs...you'll be a man my son!" The Army teaches you to be passionate *and* to master your passion.

The Apprentice

I really enjoyed working with John on tasks. He was always intense, but John got extremely passionate about one of our tasks. In what was a real challenge, our team had to choose a clothing designer, work with her to create some outfits, and stage a full fashion show featuring our new line. John felt very strongly that the designer he selected and the line we developed were both creative, daring, and cutting edge. He felt that his vision perfectly embodied our mission: which was, after all, to create a fashion line.

Most people who saw the show would agree, I think, when they saw our line versus the women's line, that the men's team really captured the look and feel of a true runway show in Paris. Ours were very exaggerated designs, to highlight the concept. The women's line, on the other hand, was a collection that buyers from Macy's could place an order for on the spot. Their designs didn't need to be toned down or adapted to make them work for a mass audience. And the retailers who attended the show put a lot more orders in for the women's designs than for ours. So we lost.

John really stuck to his guns; his passion was absolute. There's no denying he did a great job; unfortunately, our success was measured in terms of dollars by the number of sales, and the buyers could not buy our line exactly as it was. We lost, but in the Boardroom, I admired John for saying, "I'm not going to apologize for being passionate about this vision." He really was, and that came through loud and clear.

My youngest brother Brent served as an Army officer in Iraq, doing some of the most dangerous work that can be done. Fortunately, he came home unharmed, and so did all his men. He is now a bond trader at Lehman Brothers in New York, and he told me about his employer's concern when he first started work:

"Working as a trader is considered a very stressful job by some. There are times the trading floor gets a little crazy, but I spent the good part of seven years getting yelled at by some very tough guys. When I get yelled at here, I can take it very well. In fact, when I first started on my desk, my supervisors were a little concerned that I didn't get fired up enough when everything around me was heating up. No matter what happened, I would just say, "OK," put my head down, and keep on with my work.

"Part of the training process was to determine every new employee's threshold, and there were several new people who just freaked out and walked off the floor. I always took whatever was thrown at me and said, 'I got it.' I remained perfectly calm and focused on my job. Something I always liked to say in the Army—and still do—is that any one person can only do so much. I have two hands and one head, and the only thing I can do is my best. If you're giving 100 percent and doing the best you can with what you've got, people can't ask much more of you.

> Only passions, great passions, can elevate the soul to great things.
>
> —DENIS DIDEROT

"This calm and focus at work is part of what serving in the military has done for me. I really don't take things seriously that don't need to be taken seriously. At the end of my days now, no one is shooting at me, and I'm going home to sleep in my bed. How bad can anything else get? I was deployed to Iraq and put in charge of other people's lives. It really puts everything in its proper perspective."

Take a look at any season of *The Apprentice* and you'll see people losing their cool—and how that has detrimental effects on performance. In the military, stress or pressure is no excuse for losing control and making bad decisions. That kind of passion, in the military, is only proof that you don't have what it takes to be a leader, because you've lost control of yourself and, inevitably, others.

On *The Apprentice* and in my businesses I've always tried to harness people's passions while reining in emotions that would have disrupted their performance. One of our tasks on *The Apprentice* was setting up a bridal shop. Sandy was clearly an expert in the field—she owned her own bridal shop! She was the perfect person to have on our team. She had passion, knowledge, and experience. But I was careful not to let the team make Sandy the project manager. Leaders should lead, and let experts focus on the thing they love. It's a mistake to let the subject matter expert lead, rather than a business executive. Otherwise there is no one to keep the experts' passion properly harnessed and directed. Now, you can't always give someone something to do that they are passionate about. Not all tasks are fun! But that's why you surround yourself with great people—they know that sometimes the work won't be fun, but if you give them something they love to do frequently, you'll keep people excited.

> Be still when you have nothing to say; when genuine passion moves you, say what you've got to say, and say it hot.
>
> —D. H. LAWRENCE

The competing team on the bridal task pretty much gave up. We didn't witness it, of course, I only saw it on the show like everyone else, but it appeared that by having an expert on our team it completely demoralized them right from the start. They got into the mindset right away of, "We're never going to beat those guys; they have Sandy." That is not the way to lead troops. Yes, you need to be realistic about what you're facing and the capabilities of the competition. But you never want to come to the foregone conclusion that you've lost at the beginning. That will never inspire passion in your troops, or your employees.

Employees are just like soldiers. They look to you for vision and guidance. You better have some passion to go along with it, or they'll see right through you. And you won't be very effective, and you won't ever win.

After I won *The Apprentice* I was given the opportunity to run the live auction the Larry King Heart Foundation gala. One of the most coveted auction items that night was a personal portrait painted by renowned artist Peter Max. Peter is one of the best examples I've ever seen of marrying passion with a business sense. A true artist, he is passionate about creative expression in all mediums: oils, acrylics, pastels, engravings, animation cells, you name it, and it's served as a canvas for his expression. He had a magical childhood, full of adventure, living in a pagoda hut in Shanghai, China, for the first ten years of his life. His parents later took him to India, Africa, and Israel, where Peter started to study art and astronomy, another lifelong passion.

From reading American comic books, hearing radio broadcasts, and seeing American films, the young Peter formed a vision of America as a place full of swashbuckling heroes in the land of freedom. In 1953, he emigrated with his parents to the United States and studied at the Art Students League in Manhattan. Fascinated with the latest trends in commercial illustration, graphic arts, and photography, he became known for his instantly recognizable style.

A true sixties icon, he studied meditation and the spiritual teachings of the East with an Indian yoga master.

What's so fascinating about Peter is that he marries pragmatism to passion as a commercial artist. He produces and sells original artwork at a prolific rate and enhances his earnings by authorizing signed prints of his work. His fame and accomplishments are amazing: he has painted four presidents, been the official artist for five Super Bowls, designed the first ten-cent stamp and the famous Love stamp, appeared on the cover of *Life*, painted an airplane in his signature style, and published art books. Still, he continues to work hard every day, and does a tremendous amount of charitable work. Some artists and critics, however, have taken him to task for "selling out"—an accusation I can't understand at all. By combining passion with pragmatism, what he really is . . . is successful.

When I began work as an official employee of the Trump Organization I was charged with three projects. 40 Wall Street was a 1.3 million square foot commercial office building that Donald Trump purchased in the 1990s. He believed ten years ago when he bought that building that the downtown area of New York would someday make a comeback. He knew that he could do to this property what he does to all his properties: fix it up, remake it inside and out, put in all the best amenities, and have a new "Trump" building. He was right: 40 Wall Street is now a premiere Manhattan office building with such anchor tenants as American Express. 40 Wall Street is now worth hundreds of millions of dollars. My job was to learn and to help manage the property.

I worked very closely with George Ross on this project. George quickly became an amazing mentor to me inside the Trump

Organization. With fifty-plus years experience as an attorney, nego-
tiator, and real estate expert, I couldn't have asked for a more valuable ally, mentor, and tutor.

My other real estate project was residential. Trump Tower Tampa
came about when a land developer called SIMDAG in the Tampa,
Florida, area approached Donald Trump about partnering with him
in a luxury high-rise condominium building. They proposed a towering fifty-story building with more than 190 units, ten stories
higher than any other building on the west coast of Florida. They
wanted the signature Trump appeal for their project: the sheer size,
grandeur, quality, and amenities that would turn their building into
a Trump property and appeal to luxury home buyers.

The Trump team did their due diligence on both the developer
and the demographics of the area. In the course of doing this homework, the team discovered that Tampa had plenty of residents desir-
ing a higher standard of living: concierge service, valet parking,
touch-screen ordering and delivery from restaurants in the building,
and so on. Again, this is another perfect example of Donald Trump's
vision. This was a project many people believed couldn't be done.
Many questioned whether the area had enough demand for very
high-end condominiums—with starting prices of $700,000 going all
the way to over $5 million. Mr. Trump and his team believed that
there was enough demand to support such a project, and once again
he was right.

On my first day of work, Donald asked me to assist with the sales
and marketing of the new units. I appeared on local Tampa television and radio shows and worked closely with the developer partner to promote this new project—a task made much easier because

I had just won *The Apprentice* and had a bit of celebrity appeal. A month later, when we had the sales kick-off party on the site of the new building, we had reservations on over 90 percent of the units in the building with backup reservations on many of them. This project certainly reinforced for me the power of the Trump brand, and made me think about other ways to capitalize on it. Trump Tower Tampa is definitely a testament to both Donald Trump's real estate brilliance and the marketing capabilities of his organization.

That Donald Trump is an incredible visionary in real estate is a fact known all over the business world. My particular challenge when I joined the Trump Organization was to carve out an area that could be all my own. My background is not in real estate, nor am I an expert in that field. I knew I would spend much of my first year as an apprentice getting up to speed on many of the complexities of real estate. Learning is always exciting for me, but I didn't want to be the person in the group who knew the least. When you're in that kind of position, it's difficult to show what you're actually capable of doing and how you can perform, which I was anxious to do for Donald.

So I looked around, and one of the projects I noticed was Trump Ice, the Trump brand of bottled water served in the Trump Atlantic City casinos. I offered to take on the marketing of Trump Ice. My aim was to triple the number of distributors, add bottlers, and set up a website so people could buy it online. This would be something I could point to at the end of the year and say, "Here is something tangible that I've accomplished."

All three projects—40 Wall Street, Trump Tower Tampa, and Trump Ice—were very absorbing. As time went on, probably the most exciting and gratifying aspect for me about working for Donald Trump was learning just how entrepreneurial he really is, he encourages entrepreneurial thinking. I can walk into his office with new ideas whenever I want to. Sure, there's usually a line of people waiting, but he'll always say, "Come on in. What do you have for me. Let's talk."

After brainstorming with two partners who had strong backgrounds in direct marketing, I presented an idea for a new business to Donald: Trump Direct Media, a celebrity-endorsed direct marketing piece for premium brands. The idea is similar to the Val-Pak that many people receive in the mail at home, an envelope filled with coupons from local advertisers—everyone from carpet cleaners to picture framers. Trump Direct Media is the same basic concept, but designed as a direct marketing channel for premium brands, not the local hardware store. The mail piece offers special incentives from high-end companies—everything from Sony flatscreen televisions to Godiva chocolates to Ruth's Chris Steakhouse. Plus the mailer directs readers to the Trump Exclusives website, the 5th Avenue Club, a sweepstakes, editorial content on the Trump lifestyle, and information on a charity each month.

In a nutshell, Trump Direct Media allows Donald Trump to bring the crème de le crème in quality goods and services to select households (those with an income of $100,000 and above). This was the perfect business to integrate all that I've learned about marketing and branding since I joined the Trump Organization with my passion for starting and growing new companies. Donald Trump liked the idea, and we're off and running!

• • •

Pete Dawkins on Passion and Vision

No matter how lowly or modest your goal, you will be far more effective if you can communicate a vivid vision of it.

There's a story about World War II that, when the fighting in Europe ended, there were suddenly several million soldiers stationed all over the continent with virtually nothing to do. It was going to take six months, or more, to get all the soldiers home by ship; so these grizzled combat veterans—a pretty gruff lot, by the way—found themselves sitting around, bored.

In the interest of improving morale, the field army commander put out an official directive that, from that day on, every mess hall was required to have a "stockpot" on the stove. The idea was that doing so would allow the cooks to add some flavor to the bland rations the soldiers were being served, and make the meals more palatable. The directive went out Army-wide but predictably, given the circumstances, almost no one responded, and almost no stockpots appeared on stoves.

A young, newly-arrived first lieutenant had the misfortune of being given responsibility to implement the stockpot directive throughout the entire Field Army area. Faced with a seemingly impossible task, he took a very unconventional—but ultimately very effective—approach. He commandeered a Jeep, painted it, and put a special personally designed insignia on it. (At that time, by the way, anyone seen driving around in a jeep raised eyebrows, because there were relatively few jeeps available, and almost no gasoline, anywhere in Europe.)

The lieutenant then designed his own uniform (obviously, strictly against regulations) including jodhpurs, boots and a chrome helmet—he almost looked like General Patton—and tore around throughout the units of the Field Army. His routine was to drive up, jump from the jeep, stride into the mess hall with a chromed soup-ladle as a "swagger stick," look for the stockpot, roll up his sleeve, stick the chromed ladle deep into the pot, taste it, spit it out, jump back into his jeep, and abruptly drive off.

Witnessing this totally bizarre show was the single most lively, unexpected, irreverent happening most of the soldiers had seen in weeks. It caught their fancy. It became the "talk of the town." Before long, troops began clamoring for him to come to *their* mess hall! The "mystery" lieutenant had become an instant phenom! A military pop star, of sorts.

The lesson: Very soon, in a wide-ranging array of units throughout the entire Field Army, every single mess hall had a stockpot up and running. A young lieutenant, by creating a vivid "stockpot" image, was able to get done what a 4-star general, with all his stature and authority, had not been able to do.

TAKE COMMAND: PASSION

Align your passion and your "work." Excitement is contagious and it will be apparent to all of those around you. Success will follow.

CHAPTER FOUR

Perseverance: It's Not the Size of the Dog in the Fight; It's the Size of the Fight in the Dog

If there is one quality any entrepreneur needs to have, it's perseverance. In my opinion, there are two key traits that epitomize an entrepreneur. Passion is the driving force, but I cannot emphasize enough the importance of having the ability to "keep on keeping on" when everyone above you, below you, and around you has fallen by the wayside. Leaders never say die and never stop moving forward. It's critical.

Donald Trump is the absolute perfect example of perseverance. Look at the very first deal he did in 1974, when he was just twenty-five years old. He saw a huge, rundown old building, a real eyesore, right next to Grand Central Station. The building had formerly been the Commodore Hotel, and Donald envisioned a brand-new, first class convention hotel that would revitalize the entire neighborhood. Everybody watching him try to put together this deal just shook their heads, wondering what he could possibly be thinking. The obstacles in his way were overwhelming. New York City itself was facing bankruptcy, and the State of New York had no money to contribute to the venture. Penn Central, a bankrupt railroad company, held the lease on the building but owed millions of dollars in back taxes to the city. Not to mention that there was very little happening in terms of tourism to New York—who was going to stay at this hotel? No hotel chain was interested in a new facility—occupancy rates all over the city were dismal.

The complex series of deals and maneuvers it took to get all the various factions on board were truly dizzying. But Donald was not to be deterred from his vision, and he persevered until more than five years later the beautiful Grand Central Hyatt opened—and it was a success from the very first day.

Donald Trump doesn't know the meaning of the words "give up." He has gone through so many reversals, roller-coaster ups and downs in his career. He likes to tell the story of going out for a walk one afternoon with his daughter Ivanka. As they approached the Trump Building they noticed a homeless man lying in the street. "See that guy over there?" he asked Ivanka.

> Victory belongs to the most persevering.
>
> —NAPOLEON BONAPARTE

"He's wealthier than I am." He wasn't kidding—at the time, he was in debt to the tune of $900 million. That's what can happen when you're leveraged.

But he persevered, looked for a way out, envisioned possible solutions, used all of his skills, and called on every one of his contacts. Eventually, he restructured the debt and kept moving forward. Now, it would have been quite easy to give up in that situation. But he chose to persevere—because to him, there's just no other option. And his success, riches and reputation came back twice as strong. Now he's back on top of the world, but he hasn't forgotten the ups and downs of his journey, and he wants his employees to share his determination. In a television interview Donny Deutsch recently asked Donald Trump what trait the first three Apprentices—meaning Bill, Kendra, and I—all had in common. His answer was: "Their never-say-die attitude." Clearly, perseverance was a key factor in my being hired.

Anyone who makes it through the first year of West Point knows what perseverance is. Almost every cadet came from a high school where he was a "big man on campus." They were captains of their teams, presidents of their classes, National Merit scholars. In high school, they had grown accustomed to being at the top of the heap. West Point was a much tougher proving ground. And believe me, it was a proving ground.

West Point fostered a tremendously competitive environment. Every single week from the moment I arrived, my rank in my class was listed on a wall. There were about 1,300 cadets in my starting class (although closer to 1,000 actually graduated) and we were listed out by name and ranked from #1 to #1,300 starting the very first week. Our ranking was based on a mixture of academics, military bearing, and physical requirements, with the various factors being weighted and combined to come up with our overall rank, which was posted in public each week. Our ranking was what determined our eventual branch posting after graduation. The lowest-ranked person in the class is known as the Goat, and at graduation everyone in the class has to give him or her a dollar. General Patton wasn't the goat of his class, though he struggled a bit. The joke is the powers that be placed his statue facing the West Point library because it was rumored he never went there! (Though anyone who knows anything about Patton knows he was an avid reader of military history.)

As a West Point plebe I was required to take twenty credit hours of classes per semester—every student graduated with 164 credits. A normal Bachelor of Science degree is, I believe, usually about 128 credits. So in terms of academic work alone, everyone was completely overloaded. There were classes on Saturday and tremendous amounts of homework—the academic program was extremely challenging.

Then, of course there was the military training, and every Saturday we put on a parade for the public. Plus, each cadet was required to participate in athletics—no opting out. If you did not play a varsity sport, you had to play intramurals, and those intramurals were tough. From what I could gather, they were pretty much the equivalent to every other college's junior varsity programs. Many athletes who couldn't get into a Division I-A school on a sports scholarship wound up at West Point.

In addition to classes, drill and sports, there was the whole detail of running the Academy. Plebes delivered all the upperclassmen's mail and laundry and called out the details of every formation. "Ten minutes until dinner formation! Uniform A!" Under every clock in every hallway of West Point stood a freshman yelling out the minutes until formation, giving upperclassmen the information they needed on what to wear and when to be there. This ensured that everyone showed up in formation, on time, wearing the correct uniform. It was also a chance to exercise your command voice—the voice you use when in front of a large number of soldiers so that they can all hear you. And your memory was sure to be quizzed by upperclassmen that happened by.

The first few days at West Point were a blur of processing: getting our books and our uniforms, figuring out where the mailroom was, and getting used to sharing a room with three other plebes. Just for starters, we were all trying to adjust to walking at the correct military pace—two steps per second—or "pinging" as it was commonly referred to by upperclassmen. I might be headed down the hallway and if I slowed down for whatever reason, even for a second, and was seen by an upperclassman all of a sudden I would hear: "Hey Mister! You better *move out!*"

We all quickly learned how to stand straight, thumbs down, aligned with the seams of our trousers. We learned to stand at attention, stand at-ease, how to salute upperclassmen, and how to address upper-

> Great works are performed not by strength, but perseverance.
>
> —SAMUEL JOHNSON

classmen properly. There were no radios or music allowed in the first year. We weren't allowed to have cars. We got 4 to 5 hours of sleep a night—maybe 6 on a good night. As plebes, we were only allowed to leave campus two weekends the first year. And that was only once you proved that you were academically and militarily proficient.

Everything had changed...Hair: it was gone, shaved off. Uniforms: no more civilian clothes. Suddenly, everyone looked exactly the same. New language: every sentence now ended in "Sir" or

"Ma'am"—and you didn't speak unless you were spoken to first. Bed: a quarter must bounce off it after it's made, and every bunk needs to look the same. Cleanliness: No dust or dirt anywhere, ever—inspections could happen at any time.

Obviously, this new routine was shocking to anyone who had never been exposed to a military environment. Certainly there were a lot of late-nights waiting in line at the pay phone with first-year students calling home and crying to mommy and daddy. For the plebes, the first couple of weeks are a rude and disorienting shock. Plenty of people washed out that first month. They just couldn't take it. And that's fine, it's exactly what the program is designed for—to weed out those who can't adapt and who crumple under pressure. Personally, I relished the challenge, although I'm sure my Mom and Dad remember just a few stressed-out calls from me during that first month!

> Courage and perseverance have a magical talisman, before which difficulties disappear and obstacles vanish into air.
>
> —JOHN QUINCY ADAMS

I shared a room with three other plebes, and I made fast friends with a guy from Long Island, New York, named Nazarro Propati (but we all called him "Zarro"). Although leave from post was extremely restricted that first year, his family lived near enough to come see him on weekends whenever family visits were allowed. His parents used to bring us great food. His mom baked chocolate chip cookies and mouthwatering Italian dishes for us, and the couple of days we were allowed to leave for very short periods of time, Zarro invited me to come with him. His family was very gracious, and I appreciated them offering me a little sense of home. There was no way I had the time to go all the way back to Wyoming to visit my Dad or Florida to see my Mom.

Zarro eventually decided that he was just not cut out for all the strict discipline and constantly being told what to do. He took a hard look ahead into the future and asked himself, "Do I want to spend the next three years in this type of institution where everything is squared corners, dotted i's and crossed t's to the *nth* degree? Or would I be happier and more productive in an environment where I have more control over what I do day to day? Someplace where I get to choose the subjects I want to study and figure out for myself how to structure my time?" Zarro made up his mind and left West Point after our first year. Now, his was not a case of a lack of perseverance or a defeatist "I can't do it" attitude. He simply decided that he needed to pursue a different track. It's important to know what you're cut out to be. Understanding what makes you happy is 90 percent of the battle in life. Zarro is now happily married and living in Chicago, and we're still friends.

Bottom line: you need to know yourself. You need to make an honest assessment of your personal strengths and weaknesses, realize what your capabilities and limitations are, understand what motivates you and which achievements will make you proud and happy, figure out who it is you want to please and what kind of material goals will satisfy you. Once you've done that, you can set goals, develop them, and put your passion and perseverance to work. Without self-knowledge, planning, passion, and perseverance, you're going nowhere.

West Point and the Army taught me the rewards of hard work— and that the weakest part of the body is your mind. When it says "can't," you have to have the will, drive, and perseverance to make it say "can." The military teaches us to get to that point where we have the willpower and mental control to get past fear, stress, and exhaustion. The military is the ultimate "can-do" organization. Of course, many people in the civilian world aren't ever pressed to their breaking point, or even anywhere close, but they may develop a wrong attitude anyway. They give up; they think negatively. No successful leader or entrepreneur ever thought that way. You need to know your strengths—and you need to exploit them.

As a senior, or "firstie," at West Point it came time to declare my "military major," so I needed to know where I could excel and make the greatest contribution. An infantry officer, for example, has to lead from the front. Impress young troops with physical prowess. Push-ups, pull-ups, tough decision-making, engaging with them on a personal level, getting them comfortable with each other and turning them into a cohesive, effective fighting force—it's the prototypical Army calling. Many firsties requested infantry units, because it is a very challenging leadership position with many rewards.

I selected the branch called Military Intelligence (MI), which offered a very different challenge. In that position I would be sitting with commanders, describing the battlefield situation, and convincing them that I knew what I was talking about. It would require using my analytical skills first and foremost. I thought that MI was the area most challenging and best suited to my skills and interests.

After I joined the army as a military intelligence officer, I made the decision to earn my Ranger tab. It was here that I was pushed to my breaking point, every minute of every day for sixty-seven days. I knew that one of my duties as a junior military intelligence officer would be advising infantry commanders, usually a major or a lieutenant colonel, but sometimes a general. This was the man who led a battalion, brigade, or division out there on the battlefield. I would be advising him: "This is what the battlefield looks like. Here is where the enemy is and this is the action he is most likely to take in the next twelve to twenty-four hours. To most effectively complete your mission, you should deploy your troops to Point A and not Point B, and the time you need to do it is within the next four hours."

I wanted any commander I was briefing to look at me, see my Ranger tab, and know that I absolutely understood the ramifications on the front line troops of what I was recommending. I would know from experience just what I was asking of his troops: how it would impact them physically, emotionally, and psychologically. I reasoned that they would listen to me more attentively if I had a Ranger tab, had humped a rucksack ten kilometers through a swamp in Florida or a desert in Utah, and set up an ambush using live ammo. Earning the Ranger tab would give me credibility with higher-ranking combat officers.

If West Point was a marathon, Ranger school was a sprint, but it was the most strenuous sixty-seven-day sprint imaginable. And it lasted sixty-seven days only if you made it through the entire program on your first attempt—which only about a third of Rangers manage to do.

The whole idea behind Ranger school is to simulate small unit tactical operations during combat. It is supposed to give soldiers the stress they would actually experience in war. It's a physical, mental, and emotional test. From not sleeping at all, to not eating much, to the constant changing of orders to the immense physical demands, Ranger school is the proving ground for stamina, effective leadership, and platoon-sized tactics. We were split into groups of between thirty and fifty men. We conducted missions and rotated through various leadership roles while under constant watch and evaluation.

The Ranger instructors evaluated our technical and tactical efficiency—errors might include making too much noise, leaving litter behind, giving away our position, not bringing enough firepower on the objective, or walking into an ambush. The idea behind every mission was that we were fighting opposing forces and should conduct ourselves as if in real combat, so all of these elements were absolutely critical. For example, one mission might be assigned at 2200 hours (10 p.m.). You're the platoon leader, and you have to travel ten clicks (kilometers) across the desert to a certain location where a road junction is, set up an ambush and bring fire down on the intersection, because intelligence believes that an enemy convoy is going to be there at approximately 0200 hours (2 a.m.). You have four hours to figure it all out, put together an operations order, execute a plan with all contingencies accounted for, assign and delegate responsibility to different people, and choose subordinate leaders.

You might be platoon leader one mission and just an ammo carrier the next. Everyone eventually rotated through every position, but we were only evaluated during leadership spots. Therefore, when anyone was in a leadership position, they wanted everyone to perform for them. (Sounding familiar? Maybe a little bit like *The Apprentice*?) Which meant I needed to perform at peak capacity at all times, because when it was my turn to be in charge, I wanted everyone to do the same for me. Of course there were a few "Spot-light Rangers," who would only perform in a leadership position where the instructors were grading them. In the leadership positions we got either a "go" or a "no-go" for every mission. Very simple, a yes or no, pass or fail grade, based on a whole checklist. But we were also evaluated in our various positions by our peers at the end of each mission. The worst peer rating performer was "recycled," meaning that person got held back for the next class to come through. If it happened more than once, you were gone from Ranger school. So it was quite possible to get "peered out" of the program. If anyone wasn't carrying their weight, it showed up at the end of the mission, because there was either open-ballot or secret-ballot voting on each team member's performance by his peers.

This evaluation system is mirrored in businesses that have 360-degree evaluations. Ratings from your peers and subordinates are always the most telling. You can fool your supervisors sometimes, but you can never fool your subordinates. Either you're an effective and respected leader, or you're not. The peer system in Ranger school gave a true indicator of your performance, just like the 360 degree evaluations do in business. Everyone who's ever had a job is familiar with the kind of employee who only gets busy when the boss is watching. This dynamic showed up on *The Apprentice*, too. If people only started working when Carolyn walked by, the people on your team would certainly try to get you fired in the boardroom. The difference was Donald Trump had the final decision on *The Apprentice*. But your peers could actually knock you out of Ranger school.

Ranger school consisted of three main phases. It opened with seven days called "city week," which served to weed out all the

---

The Apprentice

In one of the early tasks in Season 3 of *The Apprentice*, both teams were charged with renovating a motel on the Jersey seashore. Verna clashed with her project manager, and after a long, frustrating day basically just gave up. Verna actually left the premises, wheeling her suitcase behind her. Carolyn got into her car and searched the streets, eventually bringing her back to the fold. Her teammates accepted her back with hugs, though a couple expressed some reservations.

In the Boardroom, Donald told her that he'd heard she'd had some problems, but there was nothing he liked better than a comeback. Verna spent that night resting, but decided the next morning that she just couldn't take it. She packed her bags again, and this time left for good.

This behavior is more than a little baffling to me. Hundreds of thousands of people vied for a spot on that show, and she was smart enough, good enough, and lucky enough to land in that position. For her to say, "I'm not going to do it, I can't continue," was enough to make me scratch my head. Certainly anyone looking to bet on Verna on a long-term race might think twice now.

---

people who shouldn't have been there in the first place. Push-ups, long runs, two a.m. wake-up calls...there was a lot of physical and mental aggravation. We ran obstacle courses that had a foot of standing water in them. And at dawn in the wintertime at Fort Benning, Georgia, whoever went first literally "broke the ice" on the course. Everyone else followed right behind. That water was stagnant, nasty, and smelly, not to mention freezing. I went through quite a few obstacle courses where I couldn't even grip the bars because my hands were so cold.

During that first week anyone who couldn't do the required number of push-ups, pull-ups, marches, runs, or anything else was gone from the school. The culmination of "city week" was a forced twelve-mile ruck march. A rucksack usually weighs between fifty and one hundred pounds and can be considerably more if you're in the weapons squad and have to carry the thirty-pound base-plate for the mortar. In Ranger school, everyone is dead tired, carrying a lot of weight, and dropping a lot of weight, too. I started Ranger school at 165 pounds, but ended up at about 135 pounds. Not a pretty sight—but a testimony to the course's grueling demands. And I wouldn't recommend it as a form of dieting, although it would be quite effective!

City week transitioned into the mountain phase, which was located in the Tennessee Valley divide of northern Georgia, where we did rappelling on ice, the Australian rappel where we headed face down with our rucksacks straight down the mountain; and the buddy rappel where you actually have to hang onto the back of the guy who's rappelling—it is supposed to increase the trust level between the Ranger buddies and increase your confidence in the equipment. We also did plenty of marching. It was the most physically debilitating environment imaginable. We all had to strip down to a single layer of clothing before starting any extended march, otherwise we would overheat from the exertion of marching while carrying such a heavy load. At the end of a march, when we came to a stop, we fanned out in formation, in the prone position (which means lying down on your stomach), facing out in a defensive perimeter. We then began what are known as troop leading procedures—the activities designed to ensure the troops are taken care of.

One-third of the unit takes care of personal hygiene (including eating), another one-third of the unit changes their gear, because they're all sweaty and wet and need to change into warmer clothing, while the remaining one-third of the unit stays on security. The groups rotate activities until everyone is warm, clean, and fed.

After one long night march I was in the last group to change into dry gear. By that time I was down close to one hundred-fifty pounds with not much body fat. I remember shaking and stuttering when I tried to speak. It turned out that I'd started down the path to hypothermia. My Ranger buddy alerted the Ranger instructor that I had become "non-responsive." When they asked me a question, I could not answer because I was shaking so hard. They actually had to strip off my wet clothes and lay four or five people on top of me with a bunch of blankets to warm my core body temperature up again.

Let me add that the entire time these types of activities are going on, Ranger instructors were sitting nearby around a cozy fire, drinking coffee, calling out, "If anybody wants to quit, we can get you on a helicopter out of here and into a warm shower in a half an hour. And there will be hot chow waiting." It was a constant refrain, never-ending testing and pushing to see how tough we were and how strong our will was to overcome and complete the mission. This brush with hypothermia was one of several close calls for me, but I wasn't about to give up. No way.

When I led my patrol in the mountain phase, I received a "Go" command from the Ranger instructor. I was ecstatic because every Ranger candidate must pass more than half their assigned missions to graduate from Ranger school. The swamp phase was next, and to give you an idea of how wet it was, we felt like it was a dry day when the water was only up to mid-calf. After the first few days of soaking in the swamp water, my feet turned into hamburger, and almost everyone had spider bites and other bad things happening to them.

During the swamp phase, we had to march in a single file (called a "Ranger file") three to six meters apart. The idea was that if we were attacked, then only one person would be killed by a single rifle shot or grenade. We all tried to move quietly and stealthily. At night, the only thing I could see in front of me was my buddy's cat eyes (very small, glowing dots on the back of their hat). When we were walking in waist-deep water and suddenly those dots on the guy in front of me disappeared down into the water, I knew we had gotten to the edge of a river. It was so wet everywhere that we sometimes had to sleep with our backpacks crooked up in the fork of a tree while the water level was up to your waist. The amazing thing was that we were all so tired that it was still very easy to fall asleep—even in those positions.

Sleep was second only to hunger in terms of thing we all yearned for at Ranger school. Anywhere we could, anytime we could, we fell asleep. We would get warnings and bad grades of "minuses" or "major minuses" for doing so. However, when you've slept for only three or four hours in the past few days, all you've had to eat is one meal, and you lay down in the hot sun in a prone position...it is very, very hard to stay awake. Most people went out like a light, instantly. It was nearly impossible to keep ourselves awake. We had a guy on watch for his two-hour shift one cold night who wore gloves with the trigger finger cut out so his flesh could touch the metal and he'd have a better feel for the trigger. He stayed like that for about an hour in the cold, got frostbite and lost the tip of his finger. He was an experienced soldier and should never have made a mistake like that, but he was so exhausted that he didn't even feel it.

I saw people fall asleep walking, stumble and roll down a hill and wind up half-submerged in water in a ditch and still not wake up. Guys would be walking along with an M-16 dragging behind them from their parachute cord, their hat off, and all of their personal items from ammo cartridges to nail clippers dangling out of their pockets...they got so exhausted that they just kind of lost it. Everyone eventually reached their limit. That was part of the lesson—understanding your physical limits. And also what being tired did to your decision-making capability. You have to know when your decision-making becomes impacted by lack of sleep so you don't jeapordize your unit. We also learned a lot about our capabilities. All of us became one with our environment after a certain point. After two or three weeks of not really showering or bathing and living in a swamp, our senses sharpened to the point of being able to smell the Ranger instructors before we ever saw them approach. (The instructors swapped out every thirty-six hours to stay fresh, maintain safety, and evaluate us.) We could immediately sense anything artificial or manmade or foreign in the swamp—an important lesson to learn, because it meant an enemy could also smell anything like deodorant or aftershave.

> If you wish success in life, make perseverance your bosom friend.
>
> —JOSEPH ADDISON

In my leadership role at swamp phase, I received a "No-Go" evaluation because our weapons system didn't operate effectively when we conducted an ambush. The Ranger instructor told me that we'd done everything correctly: we read everything well tactically, when the orders came through everyone knew what they were doing, but overall, the mission wasn't accomplished because we didn't bring enough fire on the target. I said, "Well, I don't have access to an armorer out here in the swamp. I'm not MacGyver—I can't build a firing pin out of nothing."

> Many of life's failures are people who did not realize how close they were to success when they gave up.
>
> —THOMAS EDISON

Ultimately that didn't matter, because the mission hadn't been accomplished. We did everything right, but didn't accomplish the mission. You can do everything wrong, and still complete the mission. That's an important lesson in both the military and in business: *It doesn't matter how, it matters how much.* In a combat situation, if your mission is to take out a bridge, it doesn't matter if you did everything right if the bridge is still standing, if your whole unit is stranded or killed now because the enemy came across the bridge you were supposed to take out. And in business, if you don't close the sale, you don't close the sale. In the end, it doesn't really matter why.

I now had one "Go" and one "No-Go" rating. The final phase of Ranger school was the desert phase. Desert phase was conducted at the proving grounds in Utah, where temperatures change as much as sixty to seventy degrees within twenty-four hours. We were dead tired, but a minimum of four hours sleep was required the night before a live fire exercise. This was my final mission, and I absolutely had to pass the final live-fire mission in Utah to earn my Ranger tab.

I led a seven-kilometer night movement in very limited visibility through the desert. We had to set up an ambush and attack an enemy objective with live ammo. I relied heavily on two-squad leaders. I had performed well for them when I was squad leader, and hoped they would do the same for me. They both came through in a big way.

We moved through the exercise and brought what I thought was a considerable amount of firepower down on the target at the correct time, and called it a wrap. Ranger school was done. We had finished the final mission—all we had to do now was clean up, get everything ready, and have our mission briefing the next morning.

I sat up the whole night thinking and praying that the Ranger instructor would give me "Go" on that final mission. For sixty-six days I had been dreaming of real food. We had subsisted on nothing but MREs—meals ready to eat, kind of like the food that astronauts take into space. Processed calories all squished together that got old in a hurry. I was tired, hungry, and stressed, big-time. If I got recycled I would have to go into what they referred to as the "Gulag" (the holding pen at Fort Benning), and wait for the next class to come through. That meant a week or two of mowing grass, painting rocks, and trying to keep busy, then being thrown in with a new group of people who had to wonder if I could carry my own weight. And I'd have to go through the whole grueling process again—mountains, swamp, and desert. I was physically and emotionally spent, and the idea of doing it all again was bleak to say the least.

The Ranger instructor brought me into his office and went over the entire mission. "That was a great tactical move on that operation! The opposing forces couldn't see a thing. You were in position before anybody knew what was going on, and you brought a terrific amount of firepower down on the ambush as well. It was one of the best executed ambushes I have seen set up. Ranger Perdew, you're a Go!"

I was ecstatic. I had done it—and I was thankful my team had pulled through for me. It was an incredible honor to wear my Ranger tab. Earning it is one of my proudest accomplishments.

Ranger school had its share of people who just gave up. And you have to remember they had to compete even to be allowed to participate in the program. Once they got there, some just fell apart and packed it in. Now, I'm not talking about the soldiers who broke bones or were literally physically unable to go on. But there were plenty of guys who were no worse off than everybody else in terms of physical pain and exhaustion. Their ability to cope just wasn't as strong. The ability to persevere just wasn't there. You see this in the business world as well. Mental toughness is a big part of perseverance.

One of the most interesting aspects of the program was how easy they made it to give up. They invited you to do it. No one hazed you for quitting. The instructors dared you to do it. They knew exactly how cold, tired, and stressed we were. They knew how inviting offers of warmth, good food, and sleep were, and the Ranger instructors were as good as their word. If you quit, you'd be on the next helicopter, outprocessed from Ranger school at Fort Benning and sent back to your unit. Of course, you had to deal with the consequences of quitting a volunteer program where you took somebody else's slot, but you were still out of Ranger school. The bottom line was to be a Ranger, you not only had to be tactically skilled and mentally and physically tough, you had to want it more than anything else. That's why the Ranger tab really means something.

Three years into my military career, President Bill Clinton was in the process of closing down a number of military installations. The government was shutting them down and selling them off in their efforts to reduce the federal budget on defense spending. As part of these reductions the Army's forward-looking troop requirements were suddenly too much. There was a surplus of officers with nowhere to put them. So the Army offered to release officers in certain year groups from their military obligation. If we wanted to get out, we could. After some soul-searching, I decided that ultimately I wanted to use my skills in the business world, and I took advantage of the opportunity to pursue law and business degrees at UCLA.

In my third year of my joint degree program at Anderson and UCLA Law, I wrote a business plan for a company called ImageTel, and started raising money for the business during the summer before my last year of school. ImageTel was a company I was very excited about. Videoconferencing is a solution that not only reduces the costs of executives traveling long distances to see each other; it also actually adds to productivity and creativity. A company with teams in different locations all over the country could use our equipment to communicate with each other as easily if they were all in the same room. Videoconferencing allowed for a level of communication that otherwise would not occur.

The idea behind videoconferencing is to reduce costs and time lost in business travel. Too many executives spend sitting in airports, riding in taxis, flying on planes with the result that they're tired, spend too much time away from their family, and lose productive hours or days at the office. Videoconferencing means a meeting between a New York and Seattle office can be as easy as walking down the hall and sitting in a conference room. It is an absolute boon to executive productivity.

My partners in ImageTel and I had come up with a solution that fixed all the things that were wrong with the currently available videoconferencing systems. And I must say that we were far ahead of our time. The equipment provided was actually far superior to most of the videoconferencing equipment used by businesses today. Ours was the ultimate boardroom solution: a four-foot by seven-foot video wall, just like sitting in Captain Kirk's chair on the U.S.S. Enterprise. We acquired a number of blue-chip clients like Aetna, the FBI, and Lehmann Brothers who absolutely loved our product— it was markedly better than anything else they'd ever used. After two years we grew the company to about $4 million in sales.

Unfortunately, we weren't able to get enough money to market the product properly and take the business to the next level. As we were raising a round of financing to grow the business, Intel and Microsoft announced a videoconferencing joint venture. Microsoft introduced a program called "See You—See Me," a desktop application for engineers to talk to each other via computer. It was completely different from our solution, which was for the boardroom, not the desktop. But with these two 900-pound gorillas entering our marketplace, our ability to access capital was gone.

I liken the situation to VHS versus Beta. Beta is a much better product in terms of quality, image, sound, you name it. But VHS had plenty of money behind it, marketed their product correctly, and got VHS players into American households, so they won that fight, decisively. Our competitors already had significant market share dollars behind them, but our technology and the final resulting product was far superior. Looking back, ImageTel was probably five years ahead of its time in terms of the marketplace. Had we launched this business in 2000, it probably would have been more widely accepted. It still might be.

ImageTel, my very first entrepreneurial venture, was a perfect example of misapplied perseverance in the business world. I stayed on at that company and persevered far past the point that made business or personal sense. But I had raised our initial money from family and friends. Long after the writing was on the wall I carried on, because I didn't want to let them down. The result was I made some bad decisions and I learned that perseverance alone—which had always served me so well—wasn't enough. The consolation was, I also learned that I absolutely loved growing a business.

* * *

Ross Perot on Perseverance

I had never seen the ocean or a ship. But I knew that I wanted to go to the Naval Academy. A prominent local businessman who had been the sponsor of my Boy Scout troop had attended the Naval Academy, and he had served as a great role model for me as a child. My friends couldn't understand why I was so determined, but I had made up my mind.

I attended Texarkana Junior College for two years as I tried to get an appointment. It was quite a challenge as my family had no political contacts. All I could do was keep writing letters to Congressmen and Senators, over and over.

Out of the blue I received a telegram from Senator W. Lee O'Daniel offering me an appointment. I was sworn into the Academy on my nineteenth birthday. Many years later, after EDS had become a very successful company, I received a call from a former aide to Senator O'Daniel who asked me, "Ross, didn't you ever wonder how you got your appointment to the Naval Academy?"

I responded, "Yes, but I was not going to ask."

The man told me, "I was cleaning up the Senator's office one day and said, 'Senator, we have an unfilled appointment to the Naval Academy.' The Senator asked, 'Does anyone want it?' I said, 'Well, there is this boy from Texarkana who has been trying to get it for three years.' The senator said, 'Give it to him.'

"Ross," he concluded, "your name never even came up."

In talking about these events, Ross Perot calls his appointment luck. I call it perseverance.

TAKE COMMAND: PERSEVERANCE

Perseverance. Life is not easy. Some people are successful through sheer luck, but for most of us, success requires hard work—and lots of it; and the road to success is full of bumps, detours, and potholes. Face it, as an entrepreneur with a small business, as an executive at a large company, or even as the junior member of 1,000-person team—you are going to be challenged. Some times things will seem impossible. But only one thing is certain: if you give up, you certainly won't make it. Hang in there.

CHAPTER FIVE

Planning: Fail to Plan, Plan to Fail

Some people who meet me might think initially I'm a little rigid. Some of my teammates on *The Apprentice* certainly did! I took a lot of heat during the filming of the show for being so "absorbed" on the laptop. Hey, I like to plan! What can I say? From the age of sixteen, when I started thinking about college, I learned that it's never too early to start planning, especially when your goals are high ones—like getting into West Point. And after getting into West Point, I learned even more about the necessity of planning.

West Point intentionally overloaded cadets with so many responsibilities that there was no way we could ever complete them all in the time available. So we learned to prioritize. The better you become at planning and prioritizing, the more efficient you become, and the more you're able to accomplish. No person has unlimited resources; you have to learn how to best expend your effort.

Look at Olympic athletes. They practice and train non-stop, many from the age of four and five years old. They give their entire lives over to an almost inhuman regimen of training—and for what? They all have the same goal in mind: "I'm going to the Olympics, and I'm going to win the gold medal." They plan their life to achieve that one goal. Sure, the chances of winning a gold medal are minuscule. But so are the odds of getting on and winning *The Apprentice*!

I focused so much on planning—and performing—to achieve my goal of winning *The Apprentice* that I avoided getting caught up in hype, bickering, or backstabbing. I planned and did my very best to win each task along the way. Then I moved onto the next without looking back.

In any endeavor, you first must determine your goal. Then you set intermediary objectives and you focus on working your way through them. Every day I work to make progress on my weekly, monthly, five-year, ten-year, and lifetime objectives. They all build on each other. I know it's difficult on a daily basis to swing for the fence, but why not try? The key is to focus—focus on the things that matter most to you. Write them down and remember them. Revisit that list often. Break the list down into the steps it will take to get there, including finding the right network of supporters, developing an access to capital, developing experience to encourage invention. As you write the list, you'll see each one of these steps requires ten major intermediate steps of its own. List the steps, prioritize them, and then you can really progress.

You need to be prepared along the way to revise the plan as you learn more. Measure your progress, but also keep track of how hard you're working to achieve it. All the planning in the world goes nowhere without sustained hard effort to put the plan into action. If you're serious, you need to make sure you're spending more time working towards your objectives that you spend watching television.

I had a long talk with Bill Coleman, the brilliant and innovative founder of BEA Systems, a pioneer in application infrastructure software, about the importance of planning. He told me, "I'm a goal oriented guy. When I got out of the Air Force, I set a goal. I said that by the time I'm 45 I want to be running software development for a Fortune 500 company. That was Priority #1. Sure enough, in 1989 at age 41, I was the head of software development for Sun Microsystems, where we created Sun's software development process and led the development of what's now called Solaris, their operating system and the roots of what would later become Java. Right about that time in 1992 I had the same sort of personal revelation that I had when I got out of the Air Force, which was... *I don't want to do this for the rest of my life.*

"So I took a six-month leave of absence—unpaid, because I had been doing pretty well and needed the independence to reflect on my goals for the future. I bought a condo in Aspen and moved up there for the winter. I used to put my skis over my shoulder, walk three blocks up to the gondola, pick up the local paper and a cup of coffee for the lift ride, then ski all day. But after about thirty days of this schedule, I woke up one morning and asked myself, 'Is this all there is?' I had to figure out what I wanted to do for the rest of my life.

"I used pure military planning, asking: what is the objective? I realized my objective was a lifestyle. I called it 'Build a Life to Go

To.' The goal wasn't just to keep amassing money; I think that the goal for anyone should be to end up with a life that gives you a reason to get out of bed in the morning with a purpose and go to bed at night with a sense of satisfaction. It's just that simple lesson of planning we learn in the military: if you don't plan for your retirement, you may not like what you end up with, and you have no one to blame but yourself.

"The computer industry was too much a part of me to give up. I thought, when I'm 60 years old, I'd like to have built something that I can be involved with for as long as I want to work. I chose David Packard as my role model. He built a company, Hewlett Packard, that was built to last and stayed involved with it until basically the day he died. He also spent a good portion of his life in philanthropy and civic duty.

"I decided that by the time I turned 60, I would like to be able to spend a third of my time working in the computer industry, a third of my time giving back, and a third of my time traveling and enjoying life. So I asked myself, what is the biggest software problem I could see in the future of computing? And, of course, the answer was the Internet needed a new software design for applications. I moved backwards from the objective... the planning procedure I had learned in the military.

"What I knew about putting together a venture startup at that time was that the most important thing is the market you're going after. The second most important thing is the team. Nothing else matters. Because no matter what the business plan and strategy is, if you have the right team and the right market opportunity, all the rest can be figured out.

"Instead of going wide, my plan was to manage the company with only three direct reports. One would own everything that touched customers, one would own everything that touched the product, and one would cover everything else. Once I got the right team in place, I would wind up with three different people who each had ownership of an entire segment, and they'd all be interdependent. This ensured that there would be no politics. All four of us would have to rely on each other, otherwise we would all fail.

"What I had seen over and over again with large staffs was that politics came up, all the time. I wanted a short, direct communications process. I made it a rule that no substitutes could ever come to a staff meeting. You could have backup, but each of my three main team members had to come to every staff meeting. BEA was our company, and we were going to build it and make every decision together. That's the basis of a team.

"As I set about putting BEA together, I remembered a job interview I had had at Apple right after Steve Jobs was forced out in 1985, when they were recruiting me to run software development. At our meeting we talked about all my various ideas, strategies, what made me a successful leader, how to set up plans, and all that. Then my interviewer said, 'We don't believe in a virtual memory operating system from the technology side, because we don't run it that way.' That said to me that they didn't want a platform that would grow. Still, that was no big deal. I figured that over time they would change their minds, which of course Steve Jobs did once he returned and so brilliantly turned the company around.

"But the next thing my interviewer said was, 'We don't believe in having some big plan. We are sort of a self-organizing group . . . we come together and work on what we want to work on.' I said, 'Not at my company!' That kind of environment certainly wasn't the right place for me.

"So, I thought about what I needed for my own team and set my criteria: 1) My team members had to be the best I knew at their particular job. 2) They had to have been an executive in a high-growth large company, so they understood the dynamics of a large organization. 3) They had to have been executives in a start-up before, and 4) They had to have worked at a company that had failed. It's not just that you learn much, much more from a failure than a success, but you also learn the psychology of how you react, and how the organization reacts. These were my goals, and I put my team in place with Alfred Chuang and Ed Scott to form the E and the A of BEA. Then we hired Steve Brown to run the administrative functions. By the way, all of us met all four criteria.

"Many businesses find that planning and processes are a problem. It's only a problem when it affects the end results! If you have a good plan in place, it gives you a tool to measure where you're succeeding and where you are not, and you can be flexible enough to change what needs to improve. A good process is something you can measure, improve and automate, and make it easier to do the things necessary to succeed; it gives you the ability to delegate and to let people innovate. Bureaucracy is when you don't have a process and a plan in place; it's the organization's response to chaos as it builds barriers to progress!

"Anyone who has been a successful military officer is experienced with planning, staffing, organizing and directing, all those things we did in the military, the exact right set of basic skills to succeed in business. It doesn't mean they're the only ones with those skills, but they are certainly more likely to start there. It's a great foundation. The other thing is you learn a great work ethic as an apprenticeship right from day one. Not many professions teach you that work ethic. The legal system does, and some of the high level consulting firms do as well, where those first years out of school, you are working 80-hours a week trying to get to that next level. You learn to be measured by results. That's not something you necessarily learn in business. There are so many people in business who are experts in The Peter Principle, which is get in there, get something really great on your resume, and leave just before the product or service actually has to demonstrate results. So when I'm interviewing, I look for goal orientation and how, specifically, a person made something successful.

> Create a definite plan for carrying out your desire and begin at once, whether you ready or not, to put this plan into action.
>
> —NAPOLEON HILL

Leadership is key, and a leader, in the most basic terms, is somebody that people will follow. So I ask people to tell me about their current staff, what they're doing today, have you worked with them before? In other words, leaders have followers.

"What I learned in the military is the key to operational success is setting goals and measurable objectives along the way. One of my favorite sayings is: "If it isn't measured, it doesn't matter?" One thing that people don't get in building startups is that people are expert at one area that they are likely to think there's some sort of art to all the others. In Silicon Valley everybody's great at building products, but they often believe sales and marketing is an art.

They're not! When we started selling our first product, we established the process and metrics, which were quite simple. We defined the sales process and calibrated the amount of dollars and time it takes to make a sale, then we measured that every month by every sales rep in their territory. That way, we can tell you how efficient they are, and also tell you how to make them more efficient.

"Between that and calibrating the phases of the sales process and the yield week in the quarter to what they actually come out over time, you come out with a model. By the time we had done this for six quarters, I could tell by the fifth day of the quarter what we were going to book. When I left the company in 2001, we were over $1 billion in revenue, we had $1.25 billion in cash, we were operating at 21 percent pretax operating profit, we had twenty-three quarters in a row of record revenues, and we were the leader in our market. That's what efficient military-style planning will do."

The peacetime mission of the Army is to train to be ready to go to war. If you think about this mission, it really serves two purposes. First of all, it makes sure that if we do go to war our forces will operate in the most efficient and effective possible manner. Second, it can act as a deterrent: fewer enemies will want to test us if they see that U.S. forces are very well-trained, well-funded, well-supported, and obviously ready for combat.

The Army is all about planning and training. In order to be well-trained, you have to have an objective—a plan—that you're training to achieve. In the military, an officer always needs to know what the mission is. Then he figures out the component parts of achieving the mission and puts them together one-by-one.

The Apprentice

Our very first team task on *The Apprentice* was to develop a new children's toy for Mattel. We worked with designers to come up with a prototype for Crustacean Nation, a set of toys that featured a toy lobster torso with interchangeable parts. Because it was the very first episode, there were nine of us on the Mosaic team, and we didn't know each other, and there was no plan in place, which made the task much tougher. We constantly turned to Pamela, our project manager, to find out what needed to be done.

Crustacean Nation was, arguably, a pretty good idea, and we managed to get it 75 to 80 percent executed. But we definitely entered the final part of the task with several loose ends, and in the end the Mattel executives chose the other team's toy, a remote-controlled racing car, as the winner. We lost our very first task, and the finger-pointing began.

I am a die-hard competitor. I want to win everything I try for. And after this initial setback, my army training kicked into high gear. I decided to bring military planning procedures to bear on every further task. I initiated a standard operating procedure, which was basically a working document for the project manager. I solicited everybody's ideas and boiled down a list of twenty checkpoints, with beginning of task, middle of task, and end of task goals. From that point forward, the project manager, and all the team members had a point-by-point process to follow on every task. I also conducted our first after-action review (or "AAR" as we called them in the Army), where everybody got a chance to say what they liked and didn't like and what could have been done better. That procedure deserves much of the credit for the string of wins that followed.

A big part of planning and preparation for going into battle is trying to eliminate as many of the unknowns as possible. As a rapid deployment force, the 7th Infantry Division had to be ready to take off to wherever the country needed us to go. The 7th Infantry Division's area of operation included Central and South American and the Pacific Rim, and we had detailed deployment plans that were perpetually revised and updated.

In my specific role as an assistant S-2 I did a lot of preparation of what we called "battle books." If our brigade deployed to one of the world's "hot spots," we needed a full understanding of the geography, the people, the customs, the routes, and certainly the current political situation. The battle book was a briefing book for each country in which we might operate. It was meant to prepare the troops so there would be few surprises. Anything and everything from having the right medicines, bug sprays, uniforms... every last thing we might need, and need to know, if we were suddenly deployed. We monitored the weather, the climate, and even the conditions of the roads.

> The reason most people never reach their goals is that they don't define them, or ever seriously consider them as believable or achievable. Winners can tell you where they are going, what they plan to do along the way, and who will be sharing the adventure with them.
>
> —DENIS WATLEY

If we deployed to Honduras, for example, knowing that it was the rainy season, would be crucial to knowing what sort of equipment we needed and how the weather might play into our mission objectives. The troops relied on the S-2 team to relay all that information appropriately and rapidly, because the way our unit operated was largely dictated by the information in the batttle book. Certain parts of it necessarily had to be constantly updated. The general climate doesn't change in a country, obviously, but daily weather forecasts do, and the political situation could any minute.

One of my jobs was to give briefings on current events in the various countries covered by the battle books. The troops who attended these briefings relied on us to have information on everything and to have considered every possible eventuality. It's as simple as this: fail to plan, plan to fail. Not only did we plan missions, we planned the entire logistics behind them. Going into battle without having your logistics prepared and every possible contingency accounted for means you won't be able to stay there long.

When we actually deployed somewhere, I was responsible for laying out the enemy situation. The S-2 and I would work together analyzing the information we had collected from our different sources and lay out acetate over maps and diagram how the enemy might operate. In the tactical operations center (TOC) there are four major components: There is operations (called the S-3), the people who actually move troops around. There is intelligence (called the S-2), and we provided the best information and analysis we had to commanders. There is logistics (the S-4), who have responsibility for supplying food and ammo to people. Finally, there is personnel (S-1), whose job is to handle troop rotations, oversee troop strength, and a myriad of other personnel issues.

So the S-1, S-2, S-3, and S-4 all worked together to provide a full picture of operational capability to the commander who was trying to fight a battle. Having the commanding General appear unannounced at 3 a.m. for a briefing certainly prepared me for answering boardroom questions across a table from Donald Trump.

I've found that almost everything about my army training and experience has direct business applications. In all of my military positions, for example, I was graded a "one block" by my commander.

The formal rating process used to evaluate officers and keep track of their progress and performance was a set of blocks representing percentiles. There's the one-block, the two-block, the three-block, four-block, and so on down the line. Just like West Point, I was being constantly evaluated and measured.

Performance metrics are critical for any business. You can't run a business without measuring progress along certain criteria. If you don't measure it, people won't perform to it. Period. It's been shown time and time again. Now, some people might perform, and you're just lucky they do it without monitoring, but don't count on it. Figuring out what metrics to measure, and using that knowledge to drive behavior, is critical. In every business, identifying the things that need to be measured is crucial to improving performance.

If you're not measuring anything, then what are you doing? Revenue is one aspect of your business, just as profit is another. But what really drives those forces? Is it the number of calls a salesperson makes? Or the number of meetings that a salesperson goes to? The amount of advertising you buy? If you have ten salespeople, should they be spending their time at sales meetings, following up with existing customers or making cold calls? Where do you need to expend the extra effort to get the most bang for your buck? The results of all these tasks need to be measured, or else you'll never know.

> Great things are not done by impulse, but a series of small things brought together.
>
> —VINCENT VAN GOGH

The military necessarily has to promote and get rid of people constantly. In order to do that, there must be some objective criteria. So their block rating system was created. Having a random pairing of a soldier with whatever duty station they happen to be assigned to will not give anyone any incentive to perform much better than they have to. If you're never getting feedback on how you're performing, you may or may not be self-motivated enough to get the job done. Also, as you get closer and closer to the top of the pyramid, the competition gets stiffer. Of course you only want the best leading our soldiers into combat. The Army knows this, and thus created an environment where performance is constantly monitored and evaluated. Anybody who believes that they can perform without metrics in any business environment is just fooling themselves. Additionally, measuring performance can help you determine where to spend time training your troops or employees.

Metrics are the difference between the Army kind of evaluation and the yearly performance review in a standard company where it's a wishy-washy, "You're doing well" or "You're not doing well." What does that mean? How do you take that type of an evaluation and improve? The reason some employees dread this process is because there are no metrics. If every employee has identifiable metrics, they know what is going to occur, and if they know what's being measured and evaluated, the only reason to ever be uncomfortable in a performance review is because they're not performing. As an employer you never want employees who don't perform, but you certainly don't want employees who don't perform because they're confused. You need to set the boundaries and expectations very clearly. Doing that is critical to success.

Now, all of this isn't 100 percent the boss's responsibility. You are the only one who is in charge of your career. If you're not clear on what your metrics are, find out. Right away. It's not anybody else's responsibility. Go talk to your supervisor and say, "Here are the ten things I am working on. These are my goals for the next year. Do you agree with this plan and that these areas are what I will be judged on?" That makes it very easy—for both of you.

Look at the organizations that are performing the best—in any area—and you'll find they are constantly evaluating and measuring. Bill Coleman of BEA Systems and Marty Evans, CEO of the Red Cross, are great examples. In a typical small business, you should measure it all: How many customers have the sales reps met with? How many different products did they push on each call? How many units did they sell each month? What's the inventory turn? How long does it take to stock new products or reorder old ones? Measure it all, and establish standards and priorities.

As an entrepreneur you are working to create value and give investors a return on their money, and you are more likely to attract investors if you can give them metrics that monitor your progress as part of your business plan. Your business plan will contain financial projections that answer such questions as: What is reasonable in terms of growth? What type of infrastructure is required to support these growth metrics? What are the profit levels at year one, year three, and year five? If you don't have all those pieces in place, why should someone give you ten million dollars?

I worked on many business plans at Anderson Business School. We all learned the mechanics of writing a proper plan. I knew what a business plan should look like, but I certainly learned that writing one for a class and doing one for myself and a real business were two completely different things. One is theoretical, and one's what you have to put into practice. During the process of writing a business plan you actually learn more about your business and your objectives. It forces you to get right down to the basics of: these are the resources I have, they will last this long, and to launch the product I must have X, Y, and Z. You set up metrics that allow you to grade yourself on how you're doing; you learn to forecast strategic scenarios so you will be prepared for changes in the market and for the inevitability that something will go wrong, eventually. If you plan ahead, you are much less likely to get blindsided.

A business plan is not written and then stored away in a safe somewhere. It's a living document that evolves and changes with your business. As new competitors enter the arena, as the marketplace changes, as new technology becomes available, your company will change. So you must constantly adjust and modify your plan. Without a plan, you're going nowhere.

TAKE COMMAND: PLANNING

Fail to plan, plan to fail. It really is that simple. Personally, professionally, financially, you name it, you need a plan. Setting your goals and then figuring out the steps to accomplishing each of them takes discipline and a conscious effort. Do you think that the Red Cross just happened to be ready to respond so well to Hurricane Katrina? No way. Marty Evans worked diligently with her staff for just such an emergency. Where do you want to be in one, five, and ten years? How are you going to get there? Start planning now.

CHAPTER SIX

Teamwork: There Is No "I" in Team

I played team sports the whole time I was growing up, from soccer to football to baseball and basketball. You name it, I played it. I played Little League baseball from a very young age, and I joined the Ringling Redskin football team in Sarasota, Florida, when I was about ten. I used to ride my bike in full football gear to practice after school and on weekends. Coach Smitty was our volunteer coach, and he instilled in us the power of teamwork, which was how we—not necessarily the strongest or the fastest kids—were able to win some games.

Every once in awhile my name or picture would appear in the local paper, which was always a thrill. I never forgot how it made me feel. In fact, that memory was part of the passion I brought to growing eteamz. I wanted every kid, everywhere, to make the paper.

And I wanted to encourage more kids to play sports, because it's great training for business and for life. After graduate school I coached fourth and fifth graders in Los Angeles, because I am a firm believer that team sports build confidence, foster a healthy spirit of competition, and teach cooperation. Team sports are also an ideal way to learn about sportsmanship and how to be a gracious loser. Though my teams, of course, rarely lose.

To me, one of the most attractive aspects of West Point was its strong emphasis on sports. I'm a big believer in the concept of "the whole person." I wanted much more out of college than mere book learning. The physical requirements of soldiering plus the mandatory sports requirement were ideal for me. I had lettered as a varsity player in four sports in high school and been captain of the basketball team, and I was eager to keep on playing at West Point. So I played all the intramurals I could. Softball, soccer, basketball, and racquetball as my club sport. West Point was full of outstanding athletes, and they were extremely aggressive and competitive. At West Point, intramural games really were the "fields of friendly strife."

> When you're part of a team, you stand up for your teammates. Your loyalty is to them. You protect them through good and bad, because they'd do the same for you.
>
> —YOGI BERRA

The great thing about intramurals at West Point was that it was one of the very few places plebes could give a little back to the upperclassmen, if you know what I mean. On the playing field, there was no rank, and as many of you know, sometimes playing basketball or football can get a little physical. But sportsmanship was also at a premium, because we all knew that later that night we'd be at dinner formation being drilled by those same upperclassmen. Just as in business, ethics and playing by the rules have got to reamin the bottom line. And you always had to remember that today's competitor could be tomorrow's partner.

West Point gives its students real-world training exercises to prepare them for serving as Army officers. As part of my summer training I went to Germany. I took the place of a platoon leader who had been rotated home for six weeks because his wife was having a baby back in the States. I had just turned nineteen, was only halfway through my West Point experience, and there I was serving as a platoon leader for a mechanized infantry platoon along the Fulda Gap in Germany.

I had a platoon sergeant in Germany, of course, to assist me. The way the Army is set up is that a non-commissioned officer (NCO) is paired with a commissioned officer in every leadership position. The NCO basically focuses on the troops, while the officer focuses on the mission; and in cases like mine, the NCO brings years of experience and the young officer brings his own education, training, and responsibility for thinking about the big picture. It is a very effective combination, one that can be likened to the CEO/COO relationship in businesses.

I got along great with my NCO that summer, though he was much older than I was. Well, everybody was older than I was, by at least six or eight years or so. That's been pretty much my experience through life—being one of the youngest people in a leadership role (at least until *The Apprentice*, where I was the oldest candidate!) Just like every leadership position, I had to go in and earn respect through my actions and the way I treated other people. I had to demonstrate my technical and tactical proficiency, and my willingness to roll up my sleeves and get dirty with everyone else. I had to make sure that people wouldn't walk all over me, because they would certainly try. I had to maintain a high level of respect. There are many elements to leadership, and teamwork is certainly one of the most important.

Every Army unit in Germany is tested on a very strenuous graded live fire training exercise to determine its level of preparedness. It just so happened that my platoon was going to be tested on this exercise while I was there. I had very little time to get to know my troops and help them prepare for the test. They were surprised by my enthusiasm and the fact that I would get out in the mud and get dirty with them. It is important when you're leading a team to show that you can, and will, do anything that you ask them to do. It builds trust, shows you respect them and helps solidify the team feeling.

> Coming together is a beginning; keeping together is progress; working together is success.
>
> —HENRY FORD

After three grueling weeks of training we went through the course. The battalion commander threw us a curve ball by announcing, just before we started the course, that we had to do it in our Nuclear, Biological and Chemical (NBC) suits! NBC suits were made of very thick fabric with charcoal lining. In the summer, the heat was unbearable, and I was concerned that my troops might not make it. I led from the front through the course, providing direction and motivation throughout. Our platoon scored the highest in the battalion. Much of the credit goes to the platoon leader I replaced, but it certainly helped that we were able to gel as a team in just three weeks.

Teamwork wasn't instilled just at West Point. It was critical to success in Ranger school as well. Every person in Ranger school had a Ranger "buddy" at all times, and it was immediately clear that we would have to rely on them heavily. We were paired up on the firing range, going to the mess hall, everywhere—in fact, we never spent a minute apart. You watched your buddy's back, and he watched yours. There were no loners who made it through Ranger school. I was amazed—and happy—to spot an old friend of mine from West Point, Jonathan Lacey, the very first day of Ranger school. Jonathan had selected field artillery as his branch after graduation and was coming from Fort Sill, Oklahoma. I had just come from Fort Huachuca, Arizona, where I had completed the military intelligence officers' basic course. We quickly paired off as buddies during the first portion of Ranger school, called City Week.

This was also weed-out week, where if you couldn't do the required push-ups, pull-ups, marches, runs, and everything else, you were gone. No fuss, no muss, just sent straight back to your unit—humiliated. The culmination of City Week was a forced twelve-mile ruck march, and about halfway through, I felt like my body was betraying me. Actually, I couldn't blame my body—I was the one who had failed to drink enough water to keep myself going the whole way. I started to cramp up. My will was strong; it wasn't a case of "I give up." It was more like, "Okay, my legs don't operate anymore."

My body was rebelling. I was so dehydrated and my legs were so shaky that I could no longer bear the weight of my rucksack, which was more than fifty pounds. The Bluebird was starting to catch up with us as I slowed down. The Bluebird was an Army bus that followed behind the marchers and picked up any stragglers. If you heard the order, "Get on the bus," you were going to be sent home.

When Jonathan saw I was in serious trouble, he actually carried my rucksack on the front of his body, plus his own on his back, for over two miles in the middle of the march. Once I was able to get enough liquid in me and rub out my cramps, I took my rucksack back from him and completed the march. If it had not been for that teamwork, that trust and buddy mentality, I would not have made it through the march. Unfortunately, Jonathan suffered a knee injury later in the Ranger course that precluded him from finishing. However, even after his tour of service ended in the military, he continued to provide service to our country—as an FBI agent. I'm eternally grateful and immensely proud of him.

> The important thing to recognize is that it takes a team, and the team ought to get credit for the wins and the losses. Successes have many fathers, failures have none.
>
> —PHILIP CALDWELL

Later, at the very end of Ranger school, I needed my team at a most critical time, for my final task where we set up an ambush with live ammo.

One of my squad leaders came up with a brilliant idea: we could use the shadow of a ridgeline to shield our movements from the enemy while establishing a great position for the attack. The other great advantage of this position was that we could establish it quickly. Timing was crucial, as was being able to move my men securely with-

The Apprentice

The Apprentice is a complex zero-sum game where only one person wins, but the means by which you reach that objective is by operating effectively in teams. Every task I was on, whatever position I found myself in, I did my best to be a good team player to secure the win for our team.

We all certainly witnessed a few instances of behavior where people did not play well in a team environment. In fact, it started before we were assigned the very first task! Raj, for example, dressed very distinctively with brightly colored pants, a bow tie, and a walking stick. While I'm certainly no fashion critic, it was clear that he had a tremendous need to be the center of attention, which sometimes interfered with team morale. Our very first task on the men's team was to choose a team name, and we settled on "Mosaic." And by "settled," I mean we agreed that we'd take a vote. Mosaic was the final winner. Raj was pretty emphatic that he hated the name, saying it was "tooty-fruity" and meant nothing. And he brought up his dissatisfaction more than once, which was fine—while we're making the decision. But he openly complained to Donald Trump about the name after we decided as a team.

Now, in the grand scheme of things this was a small detail—but it was a telling example right from the start that some contestants were certainly more concerned about getting their own way than succeeding as a team. I thought that Raj's carping was inappropriate—it's important that every team member present a united front once a decision is made. I must say that Pamela, our leader on that very first task, did quite a good job shutting him down the final time Raj complained, which Donald appreciated.

out being spotted. I decided to go with the squad leader's suggestion. We got everything set up, and I took meticulous care to ensure our weapons were ready, fully loaded, and arranged for maximum effect.

I did not want a repeat of what had happened in the swamp, where we failed to bring enough firepower on the objective. Our maneuver impressed our Ranger instructor, and I passed my final mission—thanks in large part to the help of my squad leaders. Earning the Ranger tab takes teamwork, like everything else.

I stayed in my first military assignment—Assistant S-2 for an infantry brigade—for about twelve months. After a year, as part of a typical rotation, I went on to become a counter-intelligence platoon leader. There I was, twenty-three years old, and I had thirty soldiers directly under my responsibility. And this platoon wasn't made up of eighteen-year-old infantry soldiers, who had to be proficient in shooting a weapon and in top physical condition. I was now commanding thirty- to forty-year-old senior noncommissioned and warrant officers, who usually spoke more than one language and had advanced degrees in everything from the law to history. They were extremely well educated and bright—expert counter-intelligence agents in everything from operational security to spy games.

Once again my challenge was to gain the respect of these people who were eight to ten years older than I was and had been in the military since I was in junior high. I needed to lead them, motivate them, and provide direction as their platoon leader. I did that by becoming technically and tactically proficient, earning their respect, and taking a hard line. Any time that you arrive in a new position, you should never start off easy. It's not a matter of pretending you know it all—which is something you should definitely *not* do—it's a matter of making it clear from the get-go that you expect excellence from your subordinates... and from yourself. As part of that, it is crucial to understand and gain the respect of your NCOs (middle management), who are there to help you accomplish the mission. Show your soldiers that you're not afraid to understand what they are doing; get involved in their work and get your hands dirty. These are rules to live by when you start a new position at any company. You have to earn the respect of the people there. You can't demand it.

My final job in the Army was as executive officer for a company. An executive officer (XO) is kind of like the chief of staff or the chief operating officer in the business world. A company was made of up four platoons. There are about 120 to 150 people in a military intelligence battalion. Our battalion was forming a new company to provide better support for the brigades. The new company was comprised of troops from each of the three existing companies. As you can imagine, the existing company commanders were reluctant to give up their best people, so we ended up with an "interesting" mix. Our leadership challenge was to get these very different individuals on the same team.

> It is amazing what you can accomplish if you do not care who gets the credit.
>
> —HARRY S. TRUMAN

Managing those people and getting them all on the same sheet of music, taking what had been three different mindsets and cultures and melding them into one cohesive force, was quite an experience. We had to wipe the slate clean and say, "Don't think about what went on before. Leave your baggage at the door, because this is a great opportunity to start fresh. Everybody has a clean slate. We are starting over."

We wanted to provide them with a new vision, and inspire them to believe that they could be more and better than they had been in their previous environments. Anything that wasn't quite up to snuff before was now in the past. "We operate differently here in this new company, and we're moving forward under new guidelines. Other people might think we're so new that we won't be able to operate effectively, but we can do it! Let's show them!" Playing up that teamwork, camaraderie, and competitive feeling always works when you challenge people with the "us vs. them" mentality. This experience was a great proxy for starting a new business or merging two existing businesses, where everyone is coming from their own varied job histories.

The best part of being on any team is when the group really jells and comes together. You take five guys on a basketball court, and no one of them could beat any one person on the other team individually. You take twenty guys from different units in the Army, none of whom really shone before, and throw them all together in a new group with new people. Working as a team, together, they can perform and win. That's the great thing about teamwork: it can transform the individuals, working together, into something more and better than they've ever been. It's just as true in the business world as it is in sports and the Army. Within three months, the new company showed the most improvement in physical fitness scores and achieved the highest scores on the firing range of any company. It was a remarkable feat, and one attributable to teamwork.

A key characteristic of very successful entrepreneurs is their ability to attract and keep strong team members. I have always made it my mission to try to surround myself with people who do things much better than I do. This stood me in good stead as I worked at CoreObjects Software.

After the successful sale of eteamz, I was looking for a new exciting opportunity. Typically, I found my next one through networking. I can't stress enough how important networking is for business development, sales, and finding your own opportunities. Always be networking. Think of your network as your extended team. The more information your team has about you and the more you help your team, the more your team will help you.

In this case, I had become friendly with Ari Engelberg, one of the founders of Stamps.com, an Internet bubble company that at one time had been north of a $1 billion market capitalization. Ari introduced me to the CEO of CoreObjects, which at the time was a twenty-person oursourced software development company. Core-Objects CEO Girish Venkat was looking for marketing and business development assistance. By that time I was thoroughly immersed in the Southern California entrepreneurial network, and thought I could help CoreObjects as a consultant.

CoreObjects differentiated itself in the marketplace by being product-centric—that is, it focused on its product, rather than thinking of each assignment it received from businesses outsourcing software development as one-off affairs or projects. CoreObjects had sophisticated and experienced development teams that encouraged the client to actually oversee the process and collaborate with them on every project. Most of the staff was in India, so the total cost of development was significantly lower than it would have been for a company that had to hire and train American technicians on CoreObjects standards and practices. CoreObjects' approach, pricing, and expertise were very attractive to its clients.

It worked like this: let's say you were a client who wanted to develop a software product. You would have to hire an architect as well as quality assurance people who designed the product on the front end. Then you would need to bring on several developers to work diligently to write the code. The quality assurance personnel would keep checking it. After the bulk of the development was completed, you would no longer need the developers, except for a few to maintain the product. In a regular company, what would you do? Hire eight extra developers for the time you need them, then fire them after six or eight months? That doesn't work very well in any company culture. By hiring CoreObjects, clients avoided that expensive manpower hump. The client suffered no human resources hassles, saved money, and got an efficient, experienced team for only as long as he needed it. And the assistance we provided could be scaled up or down as needed by the client during each process of the development cycle—and always in a very cooperative atmosphere.

It wasn't that we were simply providing a service, giving it to them, and saying goodbye. Our success was tied into theirs: we had to get a commercial product to market for our client. And that product had to grow with clients' expansion.

I really liked the model. As you can see, it was based on teamwork, both inside CoreObjects and with the client companies. But that was not what sold me on the company. What sold me on the company was Girish. I'd come to learn that the most important aspect of any business or business relationship is the people. Girish impressed me with his honesty, his knowledge of the marketplace, and his ability to straddle both the technology and business aspects of all the deals they'd put together. I decided to assist CoreObjects with marketing and sales on a part-time basis. Having been the architect behind Stamps.com, Girish had a significant network of investors with a lot of money to draw upon. He had a ready-made word-of-mouth network that allowed him to start his own venture. Word of mouth is a powerful form of marketing, but he needed a more formal and defined marketing and sales plan to really scale the business.

My challenge at CoreObjects was to create a professional organization that used repeatable processes to market and sell its services. I wanted to do this while building on the company's informal "word-of-mouth" network as much as possible. Over a three-year period, Girish eventually promoted me from a part-time consultant to a half-time employee responsible for corporate development to the full-time president responsible for all things non-technical. I took over all of the back-end functions of the company—oversight of legal matters, contract negotiations, financial matters, and administration and logistics, including payroll and human resources. You always have to wear numerous hats in a small company, but my primary objective was to free up Girish so he could focus on client development. He loved sitting down with entrepreneurs and mapping out strategies on a whiteboard for using technology to solve business problems. And he was effective.

One of the first things we did at CoreObjects to take advantage of the informal word-of-mouth marketing was to create the Executive and Entrepreneur Network (EEN). We formalized a network of more than twenty high-ranking executives/inventors/entrepreneurs who served as an unofficial board of advisors for CoreObjects and many of its clients. Through EEN, our clients, the entrepreneurs for whom we built technology, had access to experienced attorneys or accountants accustomed to working with start-up companies, as well as other entrepreneurs who could share their experiences. We provided our clients with a ready-made extended network of incredible value, and EEN was a great added value factor to promote sales. It also kept CoreObjects in the forefront of the minds of some of the most creative business people in Southern California. Every month we would invite the members to dinner or drinks and talk about CoreObjects' progress on various fronts and introduce group members to existing or potential clients. This group served almost as an unofficial sales force and led to several significant sales. This was a great example of networking being an effective sales tool. I urge all start-up companies to surround themselves with great people—be it on a board of directors or an advisory board. I've seen many great examples of this concept executed to the immense benefit of the organization.

After my three years at CoreObjects we had grown to more than 130 employees—only 12 of them in the U.S.—that's more than six times the number of employees that were there when I started consulting. Of course we had also radically increased our number of clients and revenue. No one person is responsible for anything when you're building a team. For CoreObjects I recruited and helped recruit several people who wound up in senior management and helped recruit many others, so I was partially responsible for building a team of which I was very proud.

The U.S. headquarters of CoreObjects was in Los Angeles, but we had more than a hundred employees in Bangalore, India. For every project we had one or two people on the ground with the client in the U.S., who in turn shared what needed to be done with the team members in India. In an organization like this, it was crucial to convey the values, the mission, and the idea that we were all on the same team. Many of our team members were 5,000 miles away, but teamwork doesn't necessarily require everybody to be in the same place. It requires a common vision and the desire to go after the same thing.

• • •

Roger Staubach on Teamwork

Every team has its priorities. A sports team wants to win games; a business team wants to make money and be successful. The importance of teamwork became very apparent in the 1971 football season when I was the quarterback of the Dallas Cowboys. We were 4–3 in the middle of our season, until we started putting the team ahead of "Hey, what's in it for me?" If we hadn't done that, there is no way we would have ever won ten games and made it to the Super Bowl. We all put our priorities in perspective.

My teammates could see that even if I made more money than they did as a quarterback, I did not put my personal goals ahead of the team's. You take a guy like Michael Jordan, who made zillions of dollars. At the end of the day he's going to pass the ball off to a teammate. He's going to score thirty points if that's what they need, or he many only score twelve. He does whatever it takes for his team to win.

Some guys today, they just don't get it. They are very talented athletes, but their priorities are all about the personal...

money, endorsements, fame. People like this cannot be the dominating force in any company or organization. They certainly aren't the ones to lead the charge. Team players take control of any team.

TAKE COMMAND: TEAMWORK

Learn how to play nice with others. If you're an entrepreneur, there is no way you are going to be able to build a successful company all by yourself. It takes a lot of people to bring an idea to reality. As a leader at any level in an organization you have to understand how to motivate the best in people around you. That means you have to understand how to deliver orders as well as how to take them. Work on your team-building skills and always think of yourself as part of a team. As soon as "I" gets bigger than "WE," your company, your team and your relationships will suffer. Watch out for those "I" individuals in your organization. If they can't buy into teamwork, get rid of them. Remember, there is no "I" in TEAM.

CHAPTER SEVEN

Loyalty: Remain Loyal, Up, Down, and Across the Organization

When you serve as a soldier in the United States Army, the sense of loyalty you feel for your fellow soldiers is like no other bond in the world. You will not ever get left behind. No matter what happens, someone will be coming for you. It's part of the deal, an explicit promise. If you're lying wounded in no man's land, you know that someone from your unit is going to come get you—or they'll die trying. That's just the way it is.

I spent about twelve months as a platoon leader. Captain Bruce Fagerstrom was my company commander, and a man for whom I have enormous respect. He truly inspired troops, motivating them not because of his rank as a captain, but because of how he handled himself. The troops could see that he cared for them and watched out for them. He protected them—everything from when they could take vacation days to who had what duty. It was very clear that he would always push for his troops to get the best of everything.

He also did not kowtow to his commander. He may not have been as politically savvy as some other officers I saw, but I respected his priorities. He was focused on his troops and on the mission. It was just so clear to the people under him that he was a strong leader, the one they would want leading them in combat. Captain Fagerstrom was one of the many officers I saw in the Army with phenomenal leadership skills; the leaders with what it takes to keep troops moving through enemy fire. One thing I didn't like about the Army was the way politics sometimes meant that the good leaders got bypassed because they weren't good enough at playing the political game. That happens in business a lot too, where the phrase "office politics" means just that.

My dislike of office politics is one reason I became an entrepreneur. That way I could start a company that wasn't run on office politics. I wanted a work environment that was merit-driven, where everybody had the same opportunities to perform and be rewarded. I wanted to take the best of my Army training and meld it with what I considered the best business practices.

The Army (and business and life, for that matter) has something called the 80/20 rule: Basically it refers to the fact that as a leader you end up spending 80 percent of your time on 20 percent of your soldiers. As you might guess, these aren't the top 20 percent of your soldiers. Rather, these are the soldiers that present some leadership "challenges." But no matter what their problems might be, you can't ignore them. In the Army the responsibilities are greater than in the business world. As an Army officer in charge of my unit, I had to ensure that my soldiers' families were happy. Yes, that's right. My soldiers' entire lives were my concern. When going into combat, if a soldier is thinking, "We can't make our mortgage payment," or "My son is having surgery tomorrow and I'm not sure anyone will be able to assist my wife," then his low morale or lack of attention impacts everyone in the unit, and people might die because of it. If a data entry clerk in an Internet businesses is worried that he can't make his mortgage payment, it might affect his performance, but the impact on the business doesn't carry quite the same weight.

When we deployed on a training exercise for a month or six weeks, I often needed to educate my soldiers' families. Many of them had young and naïve spouses. For instance, one eighteen-year-old wife assumed that as long as there were checks in the checkbook there was money in the bank! Anything that might be disruptive to a soldier's life was my problem. If one of my soldiers had a domestic dispute, I had to help take care of it. One time I had a soldier who got his second DUI. He was a short little blond eighteen-year-old guy. When I went to pick him up I found him in the open bay at Soledad prison surrounded by a hundred fairly hardened criminals. I bailed him out.

Think about that kind of loyalty in the civilian world. Is the boss going to bail out one of his employees? Not usually. In most cases he's not even going to know about it. That idea that you're only as strong as your weakest link, that everybody's morale is so important to the integrity of the unit that you must do everything to protect it, is not something that you find very often outside the military. If you bring even a little bit of that into a business or work environment, your ability to impact performance is phenomenal.

The military fosters a tremendously strong bond of loyalty. The bottom line is: you as a unit have to complete the mission. You must have a functioning unit, well trained, that knows how to do everything the right way. High morale is a big piece of that; therefore, you are in charge of doing everything in your power to positively affect morale. And what can affect a soldier's morale? A number of factors at home: financial issues, domestic issues, health concerns. "Sergeant Smith, I understand your wife is very ill. I'm sorry, what can we do? Time off? Counseling?" There are numerous resources available to an officer to help his unit. The same things exist for employees of large corporations too, of course, but there's just not a lot of emphasis placed on them. You're supposed to go figure it out yourself. Every officer is thinking like a human resources person all day, every day.

Donald Trump would most certainly want to know if one of his employees got a DUI. Of course he would want to understand why something like this occurred, and there's not really a good answer for that. His mission is not to have an effective fighting unit. His mission is building real estate and the Trump brand. Anything that impacts the Trump brand—positively or negatively—is very, very important to him. Having said that, he and his people do take care of one another. There is a very strong bond of loyalty in the Trump organization.

Donald Trump cares immensely about each of his employees. I watched him at his company holiday party say something personal, funny, and caring to every single person who was there—more than 200 people. Unscripted, no notes. For gift-giving they had one bag of cards with everyone's name and one bag with all types of gifts, and he emceed the gift-giving for more than an hour and a half. Each person would come up, and he would say something personal to every last one of them. There are people who have been working with Donald Trump for twenty and thirty years. You just don't see that type of loyalty—unless the organization has an outstanding leader.

As for me personally? As Donald's employee, I feel a strong loyalty to him. Anyone in the public eye is fair game, and there are definitely people who don't like him and freely say so. He selected me as his apprentice, gave me a great job, and provides constant support. He certainly has my loyalty.

As Donald Trump well knows, from the standpoint of any business organization, when people stay with you for a long time, it's a plus. They know how everything operates, they're familiar and comfortable in their environment, and you don't have to spend valuable time training them. The longer they stay, the more valuable knowledge and experience they offer to the company. A leader needs to inspire loyalty, if only in terms of the bottom line. It's just smart business.

> The greater the loyalty of a group toward the group, the greater is the motivation among the members to achieve the goals of the group, and the greater the probability that the group will achieve its goals.
>
> —RENSIS LIKERT

As Roger Staubach said, "The Navy *never* leaves anybody behind. I recently spoke with an admiral who was the father of a Navy SEAL, one of sixteen who got killed when they went after four of their men who had gotten trapped. Those sixteen guys jumped on a Chinook and took off on an extremely dangerous mission, landing a big helicopter like that. Because those sixteen guys knew that they had to get out there and find their fellow

---

The Apprentice

Kevin Allen and I had a mutual respect for each other right from the start of *The Apprentice*. We both worked hard on every task. We were always the first ones up in the morning and the last to bed. I respected his work ethic. We got to be good friends, and there was an unspoken agreement between us that we wouldn't go after each other in the board room.

We both made it into the final four, at which point we were grilled by four leading business luminaries whose recommendations would carry a lot of weight with Donald: Ace Greenberg, the chairman of Bear Stearns; Dawn Hudson, the president of Pepsi-Cola North America; Alan Jope, the COO of Unilever, and Robert Kraft, the owner of the New England Patriots.

In the board room, we were pushed and prodded by Donald, Carolyn, and George. We were both asked point-blank why one of us should be chosen over the other. Neither one of us would say a bad thing about the other. They specifically went after Kevin for what they perceived as a lack of direction, because he was working on his second graduate degree. They were concerned he didn't know where he was going or what he wanted to do. Meanwhile, I was sitting right there with both an MBA and a JD. Kevin could easily have pushed their attention back to me by saying, "Kelly has two graduate degrees, does that mean he doesn't know what he wants to do?" I'm sure the thought crossed his mind—how could it not?—but he never brought it up. He just sat there and took whatever they had—and eventually was fired.

It was more important to us both to maintain that feeling of loyalty than to be chosen the winner. I respect him greatly for this attitude.

SEALs. They lost their own lives trying. That's the level of camaraderie and loyalty I found in the Navy. At the end of the day there's such a strong understanding that your people will be there for you. I think that's the one thing from the military I've tried to bring into my business today: I want our customers to understand that we're always going to be there for them."

I've actually been very fortunate in terms of working with people who were very loyal to their partners and employees. Girish, the CEO of CoreObjects, felt an incredibly strong sense of loyalty to his employees, which he showed through profit-sharing. He valued their contributions highly and gave them bonuses that showed exactly how much he appreciated their hard work.

And as I mentioned, he was completely supportive when I left CoreObjects to compete on *The Apprentice*. A good businessman understands that the best and the brightest may want to try new things, to go out on their own, to find new tests and challenges. Girish understood my desire to challenge myself on *The Apprentice*. I recently spoke at a large software conference on behalf of Core-Objects, and I will continue to do whatever I can for Girish personally and the company, because I feel a strong loyalty to both. When you provide a feeling of loyalty among the people in your organization, they will remain loyal to you even after they leave. In terms of marketing, word-of-mouth, and attracting new employees, it's a very valuable feeling.

Deloitte Consulting was another organization that did a great job of inspiring loyalty in me. My first contact with them was a summer internship between my third and fourth years of graduate school. At the end of that summer, they made me a full-time offer.

At that time I was anxious to pursue my own interests, so I thanked them but told them I couldn't take them up on it right then. I was raring to go with ImageTel, the video conferencing company, but I ended up getting into debt trying to keep ImageTel going. No one could ever say I wasn't dedicated or didn't do everything in my power to make ImageTel work, but at a certain point, I absolutely had to staunch the outflow of cash and take a job to pay my bills.

It was more than two years after Deloitte had originally offered me a job. I picked up the phone, called them, and said, "I'd like to take that job now." And their response was, "Great! We can't wait to have you on board!" They gave me a signing bonus when I joined the team and I worked hard for them for two very productive years.

> I prefer a loyal staff officer to a brilliant one.
>
> —GENERAL PATTON

Because entrepreneurialism is in my blood, I eventually left for another start-up, eteamz. After eteamz was sold, I joined Deloitte again—this time in their strategic start-up practice. That department's mission was to help large companies spin off start-ups. When a large corporation had a great new product or idea to launch, Deloitte would put a team around it, spin it off, and fill in the gaps with people who had significant start-up and consulting experience, which by that time I had plenty of.

I spent a week there—just long enough to remember why I had left the first time. And that reason was that I wanted to be a business owner, not an employee. I told my boss, "Thanks, but I've made a mistake... my heart is really in starting up my own companies." And once again, their response was, "No problem, Kelly. Come back whenever you want."

You can see why I feel such loyalty to Deloitte Consulting, Core-Objects, and the Trump Organization.

Three out of four of my younger brothers entered the military. Patrick is currently serving as an E-6 in the Navy, a physical therapist who deployed to Kuwait. Hal graduated from the Naval Academy and learned to fly choppers, but is now in the private sector. Brent graduated from Boston College in the R.O.T.C. program and went into the Army and served in Iraq. (My "non-military" brother, John, is a successful energy trader in Houston and exhibits many of these principles in both his professional and personal life.) We all know not only the rewards but the hazards of military service. I'd watch reports on the nightly news: "Five U.S. soldiers killed in Iraq today." And I'd wonder if my brother was one of them. He was on duty: taking a Humvee into the heart of enemy territory with no real protection to try and find the bad guys. At any given moment a bomb or small arms fire could have seriously injured him—or worse. It was a very scary time for me and my family—so many families across the U.S. feel this during war—and I had to ask myself too: *would he be over there now if I hadn't led the way into the military?*

But at the end of the day, that's what it's all about—putting yourself on the line for your country and your troops. I'm immensely proud of what an outstanding officer and man Brent turned out to be. I asked him to contribute to my book because his story is a great example of every principle I believe in, but especially loyalty.

• • •

Brent Osborn

My big brother Kelly is eleven years older than I am, so I was still just a kid when he went off to West Point. I remember his graduation day very well. It absolutely poured rain all day long, which is an omen at West Point. Historically, if it rains on graduation day, at some point that class will go to war during their military career. The omen proved true for Kelly's class of 1989—after just a couple of years of active duty, Desert Storm got under way.

My two older brothers served as the best role models anyone could ask for. Both of them did an amazing job in terms of balancing their lives. They were such hard workers and excelled academically, athletically, and personally. Certainly they both did well in the military. Kelly graduated from West Point, and my next oldest brother, Hal, graduated from the Naval Academy, so both of them were a big influence on me when it was time to look into colleges. I checked out both academies and was leaning toward West Point, but after long discussions with both Kelly and Hal I decided it wasn't exactly the right place for me. Both my brothers thought I could get the same kind of leadership training and military background through ROTC and still get to enjoy a more normal kind of college experience. Kelly and Hal are both very proud of their alma maters, and if they had it to do all over again they wouldn't change a thing, but they kind of swayed me into a taking a less all-consuming path to military service.

I had the best of both worlds attending Boston College on an Army ROTC scholarship. During my freshman year the ROTC requirements weren't too strenuous—they were trying to initiate us all into the program and give us a feel for military life. We met twice a week and had several training events. The training got more intense as time went on, culminating in our junior year, which was the pinnacle of ROTC. The summer after my junior year I went to advance camp at Fort Lewis in Washington, a six-week testing ground where they make sure you've been properly trained during your first three years of ROTC. An infantry captain by the name of John Drohan was in charge of training the upper class cadets at Boston College. He was and still is one of the most influential military officers I have ever run across. Everything he said or did was in our best interest. He taught us that this training we were going through was important not only for us, but for our future soldiers we would be leading. During my time in the Army, I tried to emulate his leadership style. Lead from the front, take care of your soldiers, and never get outworked. I thank Cpt. Droham for his leadership and guidance during my time as a cadet.

I was commissioned as a second lieutenant in May 2000 and then headed to Fort Knox, Kentucky, for the Armor Officer's Basic Course, where I graduated number 2 out of sixty-four lieutenants. I wound up stationed in South Korea and joined 2nd Battalion, 72nd Armor Regiment at Camp Casey, South Korea. Around midnight on September 11, 2001, I was sitting around the base watching TV with a bunch of guys. A friend of mine came running in telling us to turn on CNN, because a plane had just crashed into the World Trade Center. It didn't even cross my mind that it might be a terrorist attack—we were all just wondering how a plane could have possibly hit that building. Then we all watched live as that second plane flew into the other tower and suddenly realized what was going on. We jumped to change into our uniforms, and the phones started ringing.

We immediately increased security, patrols, and checkpoints, even in South Korea, which did not seem to be a targeted area. But every military base all over the world went to a much higher threat level and prepared for what was coming. My year in Korea was up in April 2002, so I came back stateside and was stationed in Colorado. I deployed to Iraq one year later, in April 2003.

The 3rd Infantry Division was the first division to actually cross the border into Iraq, and as part of the 4th Infantry Division, my division followed directly behind them. For the first three months we did a lot of moving around the country occupying different areas and running security missions, from airfield seizures to patrolling highways. We finally settled down near a town called Balad (along the right arm of the infamous Sunni Triangle), where we stayed for the better part of eight months. I was the reconnaissance platoon leader for 1st Battalion, 68th Armor Regiment. We had forty-five tanks in our battalion, and my platoon was in Humvees. We moved ahead of the tanks before they went anywhere to check out and secure routes. We had to make sure the bridges could handle the tanks, that the roads were clear, confirm or deny whether there were bad guys or weapons in a given area. After we completed our reconnaissance, the tanks would roll in and occupy that area.

A big part of our job was security escort missions. If our battalion commander was going down to see the head sheik of a certain town, I would escort him with two trucks to his destination, then serve as his security detachment once he was on the ground. We were the battalion's quick reaction force, on call twenty-four hours a day for 360 days. If there was an explosion near our town, or we got intelligence that there were terrorists at a certain location, we had to be ready to go within ninety seconds of being notified. I don't think I got two consecutive hours of sleep for that entire year. I would get six or seven hours in, but they were scattered throughout the day, whenever and wherever I could grab it.

My reconnaissance platoon was a very diverse group of thirty soldiers. There were several eighteen- and nineteen-year-old kids in the group, many in their twenties, plus some seasoned thirty—year-olds. My platoon sergeant was thirty-six years old, and I was all of twenty-four. Men like my platoon sergeant obviously had a great deal more life experience and military experience than I did, so I had to walk a fine line, because I was the one in charge of us all. They had to be clear that I was in charge, and I had to realize that most of the time, they knew what they were talking about, and I should probably pay attention to what they had to say. I never did anything on my own—that would only set us all up for failure. I went over every mission with my section sergeants, and together we would come up with a plan, go through rehearsals, get all the guys on board, and execute our mission. We were a team in every sense of the word, and did nothing but make sure we watched each other's backs.

I was actually surprised at how well we all got along, given that we had thirty guys crammed into a space about the size of a two-car garage for almost a year. I anticipated quite a few problems, and was pleasantly relieved when they just didn't happen. Every man in my unit stayed completely focused on our mission. Yes, it was unbearably hot, and yes, we were all constantly tired. But everyone knew that the conditions were far from ideal for everyone. We were all in it together, and complaining would only make things worse.

So, for the most part, no one did it. Each soldier did a great job of concentrating on the tasks at hand and letting the rest go.

We had completed some very solid training before we left. In terms of planning and resourcing, we set ourselves up as best we could for success. Everyone bought into the spirit of teamwork. People felt free to voice their concerns. They weren't afraid to talk about things that were bothering them. If the people in my unit didn't understand something, we'd go over it and over it until they understood what we were trying to accomplish. Many times the men brought up good points, which we would address on the spot. We did our best to mitigate any of their concerns. We had a lot of tremendous individual efforts, combined with a great team atmosphere. Many different soldiers stepped up at many times and did amazing things. I could not have been any prouder of my team.

Because we were on call twenty-four hours a day, we tried to rotate the missions as much as we possibly could. On a daily basis we might have the battalion commander, the civil affairs team, and the battalion XO or S-3 all needing to go to three separate places. Each one of them required two trucks to accompany them. I could count on six to eight trucks (out of ten) being used for most of each day. My wingman and I could only accompany one, so I wasn't always with my men. They had to take care of business on their own.

Our commander used to come back from road trips and tell us about some of the other units he passed. Every once in awhile he would see a group out of uniform, standing on the side of the road, fooling around, with no one pulling security. He would shake his head and say, "You should see these clowns I just saw." We never had any of that. I knew I didn't have to be personally present on every mission, because I had confidence that my guys would conduct themselves professionally. I would hear third-hand from other commanders, "Hey, your guys were all over it. Flawless execution. Your guys are totally squared away." It was the best feeling I could have had—to know that whether I was there or not, they would do the right thing.

We were some of the very first troops in Iraq, and when we arrived there were plenty of open, hostile militants around. All of us believed in our mission, and didn't worry so much about the overall big picture. It was not our job to determine whether liberating Iraq was the best or right thing. We believed in our missions at the time. When we got intelligence that there were terrorists doing bad things, we set out to capture them. There were several times when, after we captured a certain person, half the town came over to thank us, brought us food, and dropped off gifts. They were so grateful to the U.S. Army for capturing a person who was responsible for killing their friends and family. In the big picture it was part of our mission to help the towns we were in. Overall we were responsible for seven or eight different villages, and all these villages had some bad guys in them and some good guys too. It was not always easy to differentiate between the two, but we believed in our cause every day.

Our number-one priority was taking care of each other. We all knew the mission would get done, because that's just the nature of the Army. The overall mission would most certainly be accomplished. We were more concerned with making sure that our thirty guys and the battalion we were protecting all came home safely. I can't even remember how many combat missions we did—I think it was more than 150 combat patrols, and we engaged in numerous direct fire engagements. At the end of our tour, we had only two Purple Hearts and we brought all thirty men home. Everyone lived, so we were doing something right.

I met the best friends I've ever had in the Army. They are friends I will have forever, loyal to the grave. Serving as an Army officer gave me a sense of pride about myself and my country that I could not have gotten any other way. Even training stateside in the woods for thirty days before being deployed, we went through so many different scenarios. I pushed myself to limits that I never knew I had. I've been through sleep deprivation, where we did continuous operations for seventy-two hours. I had the opportunity to go through Airborne school and Air Assault school, where they broke me down and built me back up. I have learned my personal limits, which many people never do. Everyone would prefer to be comfortable at all times; the military teaches you to push your comfort zone constantly. As Kelly is fond of pointing out, the military is an environment where you learn not only how to give orders, but also how to follow them. How to give and take criticism constructively. All of it is for the sole purpose of making both yourself and others around you better. And everyone takes those lessons away with them.

One of Kelly's classmates was our operations officer when I deployed to Iraq. Major Troy Perry was one of the smartest men I have ever met. After graduating from West Point he also received his masters from the Kennedy School of Government at Harvard. He analyzed every scenario from many different angles to determine the best course of action to ensure success and the safety of our soldiers. He worked tirelessly though the night more times than I can count to ensure that every last detail was solidified. He could be a true overachiever in corporate America. Yet he stays in the Army. He is married with three children and besides being an outstanding officer, he is a great husband and father as well. The Army is his life.

I always wanted to be like this man—he had such a strong sense of loyalty to those around him and the Army as a whole. His dedication to duty and sense of patriotism are things that most peple will never feel, yet he lived them every day. He is only one of many men and women in the Army that I encountered who totally and completely astonished me. They apotheosize hard work, dedication, selfless service, and loyalty—loyalty to those on their right and left every single day, loyalty to their families, and loyalty to their country.

The hardest part about leaving the military was walking away from a profession that I loved and the people who made me love it. I had received such great leadership training and the opportunity to use that training in an environment that tested not only the training but also the spirit of those executing the mission. I felt a loyalty to both my mentors who had led me down the correct path and the institution of the Army. Soldiers are not making lots of money, but that is not why they do what they do. They have made the sacrifices that come with staying in the service, being away from home and family, and putting their lives in danger They are working hard every day to ensure that the rest of us can go about our daily lives. The military was chock-full of great role models—I saw so many amazing men and women who handle themselves so well. The way they respond to pressure, how they handle day-to-day responsibilities, how they make decisions, the various ways in which they manage and motivate people—it's unprecedented in terms of any other kind of career or boss I've ever seen.

The people I admire most have all served in the military. You can do as much as you want to do in the military. They are very flexible in the sense that if you want to go into the Special Forces, they will give you the opportunity. If you want to become a Ranger, they will send you. They want you to be the best you can be. And the people who are there to teach you, who have been through it themselves, are the most unbelievable examples of knowledge and strength I have ever seen.

It was a wrenching decision for me to leave. I gave a great deal of serious thought to making it my lifetime career. I really enjoyed the work I was doing—minus the long deployments, of course! In the long term, I just felt that it would be best for me and my family if I moved on to a different career. I would use the training and leadership principles that were honed in the military to further my career in the civilian world.

Three of my very good friends I served with are now training for the Special Forces, and that probably would have been the route I took had I stayed. They are currently in the training phase and will be assigned to a Special Forces team sometime in the next six to eighteen months. I think about those guys a lot and what I took away from them now as I work in New York City.

If I had the choice between hiring or working with two guys, and all things were equal except that one had served in the military and one hadn't, I'd take the one who served every time. The level of discipline they have cannot be found anywhere else, and those are the people I want on my team.

• • •

Ross Perot on Loyalty

I was surrounded by such gifted people at the Naval Academy. Rarely does God give one person all the gifts. My friend Bill Leftwich from Memphis, Tennessee, had all of them: he was a great scholar, a great athlete, a great leader, and a role model to every midshipman.

Bill came from a prominent family. He did not have to serve in the armed forces—in fact, he didn't have to work at all, but he wanted to serve his country. When he graduated, he volunteered to join the U.S. Marine Corps, where he received every honor a man can receive except for the Medal of Honor. It was generally believed by all who knew him that he would have been awarded this honor too, but the Marines have extremely stringent requirements for this medal.

When he returned from his first tour of Vietnam, Bill became aide to Assistant Secretary of the Navy John Warner. When he completed his tour, Secretary Warner told him, "Bill, you can have any assignment you want. What do you want to do?"

Bill said, "I want to go back to Vietnam." Bill did not have to go back to Vietnam; he chose to go back. He was leading a recon battalion composed of many recon teams. He had a policy that anytime a recon team got into trouble, he would personally lead the rescue. Bill rescued a recon team one day, and as the helicopter lifted off, the blade hit the edge of a cliff. The helicopter fell to the ground and Bill was killed.

My heart broke as I stood at his funeral and watched Bill's two small boys and his wonderful wife, Jane, standing in front of his casket. I prayed those two little boys would grow up to be the man their dad was. Thanks to Jane, they did. Bill, Jr.

served as an officer in the Marine Corps and his brother Scott served as a pilot in the Navy. Both have since retired. I know that Bill is looking down from heaven, smiling and very pleased. They are two chips off the old block.

TAKE COMMAND: LOYALTY

Always remember who you are and where you came from. You didn't get to where you are by yourself. Those people that helped you deserve your loyalty. When you're talking about your company, your employees, or your boss, remember, people are listening. And when those same people need you, make sure you're there for them. That kindness and loyalty will be repaid, and you'll create a stronger bond within your organization and your relationships.

CHAPTER EIGHT

Flexibility: The Person with the Most Varied Responses Wins

Any person who is inflexible—who can only operate in one manner—is not likely to survive very long, either on the battlefield or in business. Problem solving requires flexibility—and so does career planning. Very few jobs these days offer the security of knowing that you'll be there for twenty or thirty years. Every working person needs to be constantly reinventing themselves, leaving their comfort zone, and constantly, constantly learning.

Despite what many outsiders think, in the Army, flexibility is required as a leadership necessity. Officers are problem solvers. When an infantry company commander is given the order to take a hill, he isn't told precisely how to take that hill. He must determine the best way, whether it's setting up one platoon in an overwatch position and sending another to attack from the flank, or bringing everyone forward in a full frontal assault. He has to assess his company's capabilities, how the terrain and weather will come into play, and what will take the enemy by surprise or hit him at his weak point. Running straight up a hill is not necessarily the right way. Frequently, it isn't.

All the way down the chain of command, soldiers have to be flexible to adapt to changing battlefield conditions. At a battalion level, an officer tells his companies what he wants them to do. The companies in turn tell their platoons what to do, and the platoons actually execute the mission via their squads. At each level there's a creative process that occurs. Of course, some maneuvers require more flexibility than others, but the officers and units that show the most flexibility frequently win.

The creativity and flexibility of the United States military are two reasons we have such a formidable force. For example, we knew, thanks to rigid Soviet battle doctrine, exactly how the Soviets would behave in any given situation. The Soviet troops weren't given latitude to be flexible.

When I was a platoon leader with a mechanized infantry platoon in Germany, I could look straight across the border at the Soviet troops in East Germany. And they were looking right back at me. Our position was on the Fulda Gap. In the event of a Soviet attack, our survival time was estimated at about forty seconds. The battlefield was completely laid out in front of us, and we knew exactly what would occur. Their first troops would blow right by us. They had enough ammo to put a round in every square inch for six miles and walk right in. We trusted in deterrence—a variety of flexible responses to prevent the Soviets from attacking. And if they did attack, NATO had a variety of responses all the way up to nuclear retaliation. We kept the peace, and we eventually won—without firing a shot.

Employers should know that military people are creative people. Flexibility works on the battlefield, and it also works in business and in leading large organizations. Marsha Evans, CEO of the Red Cross, told me, "The more I got into my position at the Red Cross, the more I realized that all I had done in the Navy, plus my experience at Girl Scouts [as president of the organization], was tailor-made for this new position. The Navy was such a powerful preparatory step. In the Navy I ran bases and recruiting, which was perfect preparation for running the Red Cross. That's the great thing about the military: they force you to change jobs every couple of years. In my particular case, coming into the Navy at that time as a woman, we couldn't have the same kind of job in succession. That was one of the rules in those days—you had to make yourself a generalist and be able to do all kinds of duty. Having a career path in the Navy that was eclectic by design was extremely helpful in my business career."

> Important principles may and must be flexible.
>
> —ABRAHAM LINCOLN

At Deloitte Consulting I wore different hats every day, working on various strategic deals for our clients. My first project involved a team of five people to create an e-business strategy for a large Fortune 500 company planning to enter the e-commerce market.

My next project involved a team of forty people that required me to be a generalist, managing seven experts and their teams and to come up with a coordinated strategy document. I acted in a managerial and motivational role to make sure everybody completed everything simultaneously. At the project's end, I presented a plan that incorporated all the various points of views into a vision of the products and services that our client was going to offer in the marketplace.

In another case I worked closely with our client company's division manager to create a budget for the next year, review and determine which of their projects were go's and which were no-go's, and figure out how they would each impact the overall company. In that case I worked very closely with the client in more of a one-on-one relationship.

> Habits in writing as in life are only useful if they are broken as soon as they cease to be advantageous.
>
> —W. SOMERSET MAUGHAM

My work at Deloitte covered the gamut of products and services to marketing to sales to financial analysis and internal budgeting. In order to move easily from one role to the other, I had to be very flexible in my skill sets and personality, moving between high-level clients to technical experts to hard-working team members with a variety of talents and duties.

Just about the time I was starting my consulting work with Core-Objects, Jeremy Gocke, a fellow West Pointer who had graduated a few years after I did, gave me a call. He asked me to help him run a networking event for job seekers, recruiters, and hiring companies. He wanted to call it "The Layoff Lounge." The dot-com bubble had recently burst—as I knew quite well from eteamz. There were suddenly a lot of people out there who thought that a job search meant sending out four resumes, receiving three offers, negotiating for a vice president (or better!) title, and taking the best offer, all in the course of two to three weeks.

In every city across the country, these misaligned expectations were colliding with the new reality. The Layoff Lounge would be a great opportunity to help these people. Jeremy and I knew lots of recruiters, companies that were still hiring, and plenty of talented people who might be good fits. The idea was to bring all these people together in one spot.

The business model for Layoff Lounge was simple, but there were a lot of details to cover if we were to be successful and grow. We charged ten dollars a head at the door for the job-seeking attendees. This wasn't an issue for most of them. For the price of a movie, we gave them access to a stellar hiring network. We discovered that we were also about providing a cathartic experience for many of these people—an activist alternative to sitting at home wondering if anyone was going to respond to their hundreds of resumes sent out over

The Apprentice

I think I surprised both my teammates and the greater viewing audience of *The Apprentice* on the fashion task. We were operating under a serious time constraint, and were falling way behind. Our designer wasn't moving quickly enough to produce six different women's outfits in time. If we didn't have six outfits completed by a certain deadline, we wouldn't have time to get the models fitted and the clothes made. We wouldn't have any product for the show, which meant automatic disqualification. When there were only two hours to go, I grabbed a pencil and a sketchpad and roughed out three outfits. I probably got more comments from friends and strangers about that task than any other. Look, I am ready to do whatever it takes—from remodeling a house to designing dresses—to get the task accomplished and win!

Monster.com. The Layoff Lounge got them out of the house and interacting again with business peers and potential employers.

Jeremy and I looked for sponsorship dollars from interested vendors or hiring companies. There were plenty of companies who wanted exposure to people who had been laid off: financial services people (all those 401(k)s needed to be rolled over); vacation/travel agencies (all these job-seekers had been working nonstop for the past few years and needed to recharge their batteries); gyms (these people had been spending so much time at the office that they hadn't been working out). These job-seekers still had some money; they just suddenly had lots of time on their hands. We wanted to get all of these different sponsors involved so they could provide discounted services to the job-seekers.

Our model was perfect to roll out nationwide, because the bubble had burst everywhere. We created a Layoff Lounge website where a person could upload his or her resume, register for our networking events, interact with companies that would be at the events, and even set up a time to meet. We also provided an array of links and advice for job-seekers. This was received very well by job-seekers, companies, and recruiters.

As I've said so many times, networking is a critical component to success, especially in a job search. The Layoff Lounge was no exception. At the events, we conducted formalized networking, where we broke everybody (we would have anywhere from 75 to 500 people at the events in each of the 15 cities where we had chapters) into tables of ten. We called this part of the event the "Karma Club," with the idea that you had to give a little to get a little. Each person, one at a time, gave their thirty- to sixty-second personal elevator pitch while the other nine people at the table listened. The speaker then took a minute to answer questions. We emphasized that everyone at the table had to make a sincere and informed attempt to help each job-seeker. The other nine people wrote post-it notes with any leads or information they had for the speaker. This process was repeated around the table and then we scrambled the tables and did it again. And again. By the end of the night, each participant had given their personal pitch to thirty or forty people, and hopefully walked away with several good leads. What's more, each person was able to hear effective (and ineffective) elevator pitches so that they could hone their own to get the results they wanted.

The Layoff Lounge was an unbelievable success. People went crazy over this idea. It was speed-dating meets networking meets job search. Each city self-selected the industries they wanted to concentrate on. San Diego, for example, had a lot of wireless and health care workers. As more and more cities came on board, we tried a number of different approaches. We ran about sixty events that first year. We recruited executive recruiters to run some events and Layoff Lounge city directors for others. For everyone involved it was a networking win-win.

We were profitable in two months. After about twelve months we had 16,000 people in our database registered for events (eventually that number grew to more than 25,000). We had a ten-page standard operating procedure that, if followed by each city director, would guarantee that the event ran smoothly. We arranged a keynote speaker for each event and ran the very popular Karma Clubs. It was plain and simple event management. Either Jeremy or I would go to the first event in each city and make sure the director knew what needed to be done, and even run it ourselves if necessary. We were diligent about maintaining a high standard for our brand while being flexible enough to let city directors handle things once they were comfortable doing it. Even before working for Donald Trump I understood the need to protect your brand!

As we grew, we were able to negotiate marketing partnerships with online job search engines like Careerbuilder and HotJobs. It was a win-win for them too, because they had so many customers sitting at home sending their resumes in and not getting anything back. With our partnership they were able to tell their users: "There's a networking event in your city that you need to attend. Here's where it is, for more information and to pay and register, go to this site." So we had them doing our marketing for us for free!

The one problem with this business model was that we had a lot of turnover in the city director roles. We would frequently have someone who was seeking full-time employment acting as our city director, and after two or three events they would have found a new job! As the lightning rod for the event, they got to meet everyone. The Layoff Lounge really worked—a little too well! This was a very gratifying business, because we were doing a great thing—finding jobs for people who needed them.

I also got to watch the psychologies of the twenty-somethings who six months before had been CEOs driving Porsches. Now they were trying to digest that their next position would be a director of marketing—*maybe*, and *if* they got hired. A surprising number didn't have any real marketable skills. Sure, they might have had a great idea once and done some delegating, but very little after that.

At the other end of the spectrum were lots of forty-somethings who had also been displaced. These were people who hadn't even needed a resume in fifteen years and weren't real clear on how to send things over the Internet. Communicating with everyone, trying to help them all, going over everything from dressing for an interview, to how to build a resume, to how to send an online cover letter—you name it, we did it.

The business grew from about sixty events the first year to more than 120 the second year. I served as the CEO and set up an advisory board, again to get us networked where we needed to be. I set up the licensing model and networked with headhunters in different cities to launch the events. Jeremy, on the other hand, did much of the heavy lifting: setting up the website and overseeing events all over the country. Jeremy had started with a great idea. Together we set up a plan, executed it, monitored our performance, and grew his original idea into a profitable business.

Working with Jeremy was fantastic. Being able to work with somebody I really trusted was great, because we didn't have to spell things out to each other. We knew who was responsible for what. The planning that went into the Layoff Lounge was straight from the military. We created the template for the events—the standard operating procedure—that ensured the event would be a success. That's what the Army excelled at: providing a standardized model to complete missions. Meticulous planning and monitoring performance are critical to success in the Army and in business—a lesson Jeremy and I had both taken to heart.

Jeremy and I looked at the success of this particular business and asked ourselves, "Where else can we apply this model?" It was not only applicable to unemployed workers. Why not do the same thing for executives? As we ran our Layoff Lounge events, we noticed many senior executives attended who might be better served networking exclusively with other senior executives.

So we created a new model called the Executive Lounge. Naturally, this significantly reduced the number of attendees per event, but the experience was much more targeted and powerful. The Executive Lounge had a very different feel. While we did run the Karma Club here as well, we dispensed with keynote speakers on such topics as appropriate outfits to wear to a job interview and how to put together an online resume. The content was focused on such areas as "What's the next big area where investment will occur from venture capitalists?" I arranged panels of venture capitalists to discuss investment trends. A new, more sophisticated model was fashioned with the same platform, and it was just as successful.

> Do not quench your inspiration and your imagination; do not become the slave of your model.
>
> —VINCENT VAN GOGH

In the Layoff Lounge, we always emphasized to job-seekers the need for flexibility and reinventing yourself. We had to teach that lesson to all those people who attended our events. For people under thirty-five, the current average time with a company is something under three years! You had better be building skills and continuing your education—not necessarily formal education, but the education that comes from experience, expanding skill sets, and networking. Once you get a job, you need to keep—not stop—networking. Not only will it add to your value from a business standpoint, but you must always keep in mind that you might have to reinvent yourself. At any time!

The Layoff Lounge was as feel-good a company as eteamz had been. People used to come up to me in city after city and say, "This has been so helpful, thank you so much. I've been sitting at home pulling my hair out trying to figure out what to do next. The information was excellent, but just getting out and talking to other people and feeling like I'm not the only one having trouble finding a job was great." Or, "I've got two coffee dates set up for this week, and I met a guy whose brother works at the company I'm trying to get into!" This was the kind of feedback I got in every city—we heard amazing success stories from all over the country.

The Layoff Lounge worked because we had a great idea and plan that we adopted and shifted and recalibrated constantly as we saw new ways to improve it. Because that's what you have to do in business—or on the battlefield. We created a platform. The platform was training people to run events and marketing to the appropriate audience. We understood the marketing that has to occur to get people to actually attend those events and have a standard operating procedure to allow our people to run those events successfully. There were several types of customers for the Layoff Lounge. We had job-seekers, we had recruiters who wanted to meet a pool of qualified job seekers, and we had the companies who were hiring. The sponsors got value out of the Layoff Lounge too. We created value for every constituent involved in the business

In my own career, I've been flexible enough to be an Army officer, corporate attorney, strategy consultant, entrepreneur, and game show winner! Donald Trump has been extremely flexible and creative in the way he has extended his brand far beyond real estate. He's been open-minded enough to say, "Hey, I can apply the same high standards I apply to a real estate deal to a one-hour reality television show." He has expanded into a line of men's suits and accessories available at Macy's. They are beautifully done, hand-stitched, and a great bargain. I own a couple myself, which I wear frequently. Watches, cologne, bottled water—for each of these various products, he is looking to be the high-end quality provider and he succeeds. Donald Trump is the very model of flexibility. His ability to step into any role (from developer to on-screen personality to singing at the Emmys!) show that he has the ability to be flexible. His bellwether for all of these ventures is quality. The Trump brand is paramount and he ensures that it remains untarnished.

Flexibility continues to be an asset in everything I am doing today. When I was chosen for *The Apprentice*, I knew I would be thrown into a wide variety of new situations, which ended up running the gamut from opening restaurants to remodeling houses to designing dresses. I knew being flexible was an absolute key to winning. Each task required very different skill sets, and a leader must be flexible enough to produce in every situation. The person who has the most varied responses is most likely to win in any given situation. Period.

· · ·

Ross Perot on Flexibility

Life is not orderly and logical. Business and life do not follow the neat lines of an organization chart—both are far more like cobwebs. As you commit yourself to a business career, remain flexible, realizing that the more you learn about a business, the keener your insight will become about what you really want to do.

Do not ever lose the traits you had as a child. When you were a child you were totally comfortable deciding one day to be a teacher, the next, to be a professional athlete, and without any hesitation to change to a brain surgeon, plumber, lawyer, fireman, or whatever else suited your fancy that day. Unfortunately, after you become an adult, you acquire a strong need to be consistent.

Within my company, EDS, I occasionally encountered great people who, based on their initial knowledge, selected a position in our company. Over a period of time, they realized they would be better suited to a different area or field of responsibility. They would never discuss this, feeling that the company had invested a great deal of money in training them. Having committed themselves to a job, they felt they should stick with it. The end result is that at some point in time those people became terribly unhappy. In most cases, they felt that the company should have intuitively sensed these concerns that they were never willing to discuss with anyone.

We work very hard to keep a climate that allows each team member the personal freedom to choose a different career path based on additional knowledge and exeperience. If you have made a mistake in your career choice, talk to the people in your company. Tell them what you want to do. The more successful you are, the more successful your company becomes. Everybody wins!

TAKE COMMAND: FLEXIBILITY

Don't get stuck in one mindset. You can be creative and figure out how to solve any problem. Remain flexible, learn, and grow no matter what position you're currently in. You need to be responsible for recreating yourself—no one else will do it for you.

CHAPTER NINE

Selfless Service: Give Back

I'm a big believer in giving back. In high school I was a part of the Fellowship of Christian Athletes, where I got a lot of practice in fund-raising for good causes. We ran car washes and bake sales and other events to raise money. We also participated in a meals-on-wheels program where we delivered food to the sick and elderly. I realized early on that the very best part of human nature is the desire to reach out and help others. It's a large part of what makes America great.

At West Point, there was no time to volunteer for anything, but once I was posted at Fort Ord, California, as a second lieutenant, I worked in a soup kitchen during the holidays to feed the homeless. When I was studying law at UCLA, I participated in the school's legal aid program to help lower-income area residents deal with a variety of legal issues. After I finished with the MBA/JD program at UCLA, I coached kids' basketball for several years.

Through one of my good friends and colleagues at eteamz, Gary Weinhouse, I learned about Big Brothers. Gary was one, and I really liked the sound of what he was doing and thought I should get involved. So, as always, I did my research. Big Brothers Big Sisters is one of the most effective youth mentoring programs in America. For more than 100 years the organization has matched volunteers (called Bigs) with at-risk kids aged five to eighteen (the Littles), to give them one-on-one attention and be role models. You make a year-long commitment to spend time with your Little for a certain number of hours each month.

> You are not here merely to make a living. You are here in order to enable the world to live more amply, with greater vision, with a finer spirit of hope and achievement. You are here to enrich the world, and you impoverish yourself if you forget the errand.
>
> —WOODROW WILSON

The more I learned, the more impressed I was with the work they were doing, so I applied for the program and was matched up with my own Little Brother, a twelve-year-old boy named Zach. He was a brilliant kid, a real computer whiz, and one of the ways I like to think I helped him was with sports. I encouraged him to get out there and mix it up a bit more. Zach's father lived in a distant state and he rarely saw him, so I did my best to fill some of that gap in terms of being someone he could go to with concerns he might not feel comfortable discussing with his mother. We got to be good friends; it was great to have a younger brother around again. It was very gratifying to watch him change and grow.

After her retirement from the Navy, Marsha ("Marty") Evans went on to lead Girl Scouts USA and is currently the CEO of the

Red Cross. She exemplifies the trait of selfless service that is always found in great business and military leaders. "I believe every person has the desire to give back," she told me. "It's just a matter of helping them find the right way to do so.

"After I retired from the Navy, I was recruited to head up Girls Scouts of the USA. I worked with a wonderful board chair and created the idea—which captured, I think, the imagination of the board and senior leadership—that girl scouting is for every girl, everywhere. That really became the centerpiece of the way we went forward. How do we take girl scouting to girls who don't live in the suburbs, where it is readily available? We took scouting to housing projects and even prisons. How could a mother be a Girl Scout leader if she's in prison? Obviously she couldn't, so we took the girls to prison. That was an amazing program.

"We also powered up the focus on science and sports—all those things that contribute to girls becoming more empowered and self-confident. We started a number of specific programs within Girl Scouts—particularly the sports and fitness, which I think is critical for young women. One out of every nine girls aged five to seventeen is a Girl Scout, and one out of three girls is a Brownie, so it's an organization with a great deal of impact on American females. If you can get Brownies excited about science, then you can change the outcome at the high school level, which was very exciting to me.

"I loved Girl Scouts. It was a fabulous job. Then one day I was contacted by a search firm for the Red Cross job. I was interested enough to interview because the Red Cross is such an important organization to this country. I had personally been served by Red Cross in so many ways that I had never really thought about until I got deeply into the interview process. As a military dependent overseas I had taken swimming lessons from the Red Cross. I needed blood once, which they provided. While I was in the Navy, I witnessed the Red Cross in action during a San Francisco earthquake. I had had all these various Red Cross experiences in my own life that I had never really put together until then.

"The Red Cross is always there in the back of people's minds. We show up and do things when they are needed. People just kind of assume that the help will be there if they need it, and it is. Blood, shelter, food—you name it, the Red Cross is there. Who do you turn to when you want advice about any emergency? The Red Cross. We are the organization people are most likely to turn to, way ahead of the government. It is our mission to be there in times of trouble.

"The Red Cross started out many years ago on the battlefields of the Civil War and European battlefields with the idea of humanitarian aid in times of conflict. The organization morphed in this country, by virtue of Clara Barton, into a disaster relief organization. She organized a group of volunteers for the Johnstown Flood and became a very relevant person at the time. I am the thirteenth president, making the organization relevant for the times in which I lead.

"The Red Cross got into swimming lessons, for example, when it was determined by the leadership of the organization that one of the major causes of death in the U.S. was drowning, because so many people did not know how to swim. The Red Cross undertook giving swimming lessons. In World War II we were asked to take on blood drives, which continued postwar to this very day. Successive leaders of the organization added on and changed to keep the Red Cross relevant in America.

"My biggest challenge is to not only lead the Red Cross in providing excellent service, but to make good on the kind of contract
we have with the American people. I focus on ten, twenty, even
thirty years from now: what should I be doing today to make sure
that we will be relevant then? September 11 and more recently
Hurricane Katrina changed everything, in a very dramatic and
immediate way. Today we have more people migrating to disas-
ter-prone areas such as the southeast and southwest. And we have
threats from natural disasters, weapons of mass destruction, and
terrorism, which create the need for a whole new level of
response.

"What is the Red Cross doing today to make sure that we are
going to be able to respond to whatever incident may come? Are we
ready to provide mass care for the population, to provide psycho-
logical and psychosocial support for the population? That is my
biggest concern right now. Are we interfacing with everyone we
need to—government agencies; state, local, and national agencies;
and the appropriate funders to make sure that we are building our
capability to be ready for any of these things that may happen?"

When Hurricane Katrina devastated New Orleans, Donald Trump
called me and asked, "How can we get our water to the people who
most need it?" I contacted Marty and coordinated with her staff to
get more than a quarter of a million bottles delivered to the people
who desperately needed water on the Gulf Coast. Of course, there
were many challenges to actually getting the water to the right place:
the lack of fuel, the limited availability of trucks, the poor condition
of the roads, and the various warehouses' inability to take things in . . .
but the Red Cross was doing their usual phenomenal job responding

to a disaster. We were able to quickly coordinate the delivery of water in three staggered shipments to three different locations.

Because I have a strong operational background, I offered to do whatever the Red Cross thought might be helpful. They took me to their disaster operations center in Washington, D.C., and what I saw was an extremely well-organized operation. It reminded me very much of the military. In terms of feeding people from Katrina, they had served more than 900,000 meals when I visited. As a matter of course, the Red Cross had planned to be able to serve 300,000 meals should any disaster strike. At the time I visited the Center, they had accomplished their mission in a third of the time they thought they would, and *tripled* the output.

It was an absolute marvel of planning, preparation, and teamwork. The Red Cross has done a phenomenal job reaching out to churches, soup kitchens, and other organizations all over the country to create an amazing integrated network ready to execute rapid response plans for a variety of disaster scenarios.

> Love cannot remain by itself...it has no meaning. Love has to be put into action, and that act is service.
>
> —MOTHER TERESA

The other aspect of the Red Cross that very much impressed me was the focus the Red Cross put on their workers. They have mental health programs in place not only for the people whose lives are directly affected by disaster, but for their own workers and the volunteers who waded in and dealt with the aftermath of the hurricane. They want to keep their workers as physically and mentally healthy as possible so they can continue to do their vital work.

And their planning never stops; they are continuously putting plans in place in case another hurricane strikes. They've learned the lessons from Hurricane Katrina and are fixing any weak spots to be more prepared for next time. All the various functions of the Red Cross, whether it be logistics, feeding, planning, housing, outreach...they are constantly measuring what works and what doesn't in order to be prepared for the next eventuality. Because the Red Cross knows that there will always be disasters. After seeing the Red Cross in action, I know we couldn't be in better hands.

And I was thrilled to be able to work with the Red Cross to execute Donald's orders for such a good cause. I've seen Donald Trump involved in many such causes and the Trump Organization does a great job responding to requests from charities. Of course, they are inundated every day from every conceivable kind of charitable organization. Donald makes many charitable donations, both big and small, both money and time, and many of them are undocumented, like the time he visited a terminally ill teenager on behalf of the Make-A-Wish Foundation. Giving back is a big part of how Donald Trump operates.

AOL Founder Jim Kimsey started giving back when he was serving in Vietnam. "Back in 1965 I took over a team in a place called Duc Pho. All the predecessor teams had been annihilated—I was assigned there because my predecessor had been killed. Before he was killed, he had written letters home about all the little orphans running around. After his death, *Time* magazine did a little story on him, and he became somewhat of a martyr. Everyone in New Orleans started collecting money for an orphanage in his name, and all kinds of government agencies eventually became involved.

"Duc Pho was a desolate spot. I got wind of the plans for the orphanage, which they were planning to build in a big city, and I raised hell until they agreed to build it in this very dangerous sort of no-man's land. It then became my challenge to get this orphanage built and staffed. I had only the local people to work with and not a lot of building expertise. Once we finally got it built, there was no one to run it. There was a Buddhist temple a short distance away, and I finally threatened, 'Look, I'll just turn the new building and operating funds over to them if you don't find me someone to run the place.'

"Pretty soon a helicopter landed carrying four tiny little Vietnamese Catholic nuns. None of them had ever been out of the big city before, and their eyes were as wide as saucers. I took them over to the orphanage and settled them in, and wouldn't you know that very night we got mortared. I told my guys, 'Wait and see, they're going to be right back over here in the morning asking for a helicopter out.' Sure enough, the next morning the Mother Superior, the cook, the teacher, and the nurse all came over to see me and asked me to follow them back to the orphanage. During the night the Mother Superior had come up with a punch list of everything wrong with the orphanage. She went around and pointed out cracks here and holes here. The implication, of course, was that I had to fix them. I said to myself, 'Well, I certainly underestimated these ladies.'"

Jim Kimsey was only a captain in the Army when he made this happen. It doesn't matter what level you are—you can make a difference. Jim Kimsey supported that orphanage for more than thirty years. When he stepped down as chairman of AOL, he started the

The Apprentice

In what became known as "the ice cream task" our team had to work with the Ciao Bella Gelato and Ice Cream Company to come up with a new flavor and then sell it. We decided upon a doughnut/ice cream combination, and hit the streets in Times Square to sell it from carts. It was my first task as project manager.

Kevin's brother had fought a battle with leukemia and won. Kevin had actually given a bone marrow transplant to help save his life. He very much wanted to increase awareness about this disease and do what he could for the Leukemia and Lymphoma Society, so we decided to donate a portion of our proceeds to that charity. We all wanted to give back, even though it was a very big obstacle for us in terms of logistics. I think it helped us sell more ice cream, because people felt good about contributing to a worthy cause, but we had to stop selling early, remove all the signs stating that a portion of the proceeds would be donated, and get the five percent to the Leukemia and Lymphoma Society before the end of the task. It certainly cut into our sales time. But we felt the cause was worth it.

Kevin asked me if we could donate the entire proceeds of our day, win or lose, to the Society. As it turned out, Mosaic won the task, and as we were leaving the board room I asked Donald if he would consider donating the entire $3,000 or so to our cause, not just the percentage we had already delivered. He agreed. Donald Trump happily gives back—and so should every leader.

AOL Foundation and his own Kimsey Foundation, deciding to devote his life to philanthropy. As he said, "I have more than enough money. There are only four things you can do with money anyway: piss it away, give it to your ungrateful kids and ruin their lives, give it to the government—which has shown no propensity to spend it well—or give it to charity. I think it's incumbent upon anyone who's made any money to start thinking about giving back.

"During every life, I suspect most people make deals with somebody, somewhere. In school, they say, *If I can just get through this exam I'll be a better student.* A soldier says, *If I can just live through this firefight I'll become a better person.* A businessman says, *If I can get through this bankruptcy, I'll be a better citizen.* There comes a time in every life when you are where you thought you wanted to be, and a big voice asks, "WELL?" AOL had certainly grown to that point. It was time for me to give back.

"Now, the business of philanthropy is difficult. Believe it or not, it's actually harder to give your money away effectively than it is to make it in the first place! I was used to military people and businesspeople, and the nonprofit world was a whole new area. It was a real challenge. We focused on the D.C. public school system and trying to fix that. We're training new principals for the public schools. This was one of those things where you think: how hard can it be to focus on 70,000 kids? Harder than you would imagine—you have to fight everyone. But I feel the disparity between the haves and the have-nots must be addressed. Everyone needs to be technically qualified these days to have any sort of job. And I believe a company like America Online has the responsibility to narrow the gap between the haves and the have-nots."

> I resolved to stop accumulating and begin the infinitely more serious and difficult task of wise distribution.
>
> —ANDREW CARNEGIE

Much of selfless service is a real internal call to give back. In a more specific sense, many people have causes that mean a great deal to them personally because of their own life experiences. Bill Coleman, founding CEO of BEA Systems, is a perfect example of this.

"My wife and I have a niece who has a cognitive disability. We got her started on computers way back in 1983 with an Apple, before there was even any relevant software available. She was learning to use electronic mail and the kind of games and programs they had back then. Her dexterity improved; she learned more focus, more concentration, how to communicate better. Because of her condition, we became interested in using computers to try to help people. We didn't want to head a foundation that just handed out money. We wanted a foundation we could really be a part of, to create technology that would allow for a better quality of life for those with mental disabilities."

In 2001 Bill and Claudia established the Coleman Institute for Cognitive Disabilities at the University of Colorado and kicked it off with a $250 million pledge. The Coleman Institute's mission is to catalyze and integrate advances in science, engineering, and technology to promote the quality of life and independent living of people with cognitive disabilities. Talk about giving back!

I'm thankful that my appearing on television has put me in a position to do more effective giving. I've noticed that because *The Apprentice* is a "reality" show, people who watched the show now think that they know me personally. Now people just walk right up to me and say, "Hey Kelly, now about that ice cream task, how did you think of the doughnut?" Because they feel comfortable and familiar with me, I like to think I can make a bigger charitable impact.

One of the things I'm very proud of, and that I've been a bit shocked by, was the impact the show had on kids. I had no idea that so many kids watched *The Apprentice*. Turns out a lot of parents and kids watch the show together and apparently talk about its lessons. Kids who see me in New York grab their mother's arm and say "Hey, Mom, look, it's Kelly!" I hope the kids who watched the show learned the ten principles of this book!

As George Ross has said: "I think *The Apprentice* is unique because of its teaching aspect. It gives viewers insights into what does or doesn't influence high-level executives. It also highlights how people can take a diverse group and mold them into an effective team. I think that anyone who is involved or plans to be involved in a business environment can learn valuable, useful lessons from watching *The Apprentice*."

Now that I'm a "celebrity spokesperson" I can direct more attention to organizations like the National Guard Youth Challenge Program. The idea behind the Youth Challenge Program is to give young high school dropouts a chance to earn their GED while spending five months in a National Guard unit—sort of a watered-down version of basic training. They also learn a trade—carpentry, plumbing, a skill they can actually use to get a job. Remember, these are high school dropouts who are certainly vulnerable to jail, gangs, drugs, and crime, and who are headed down the wrong path. And for the vast majority of these kids, the National Guard Youth Challenge program turns their lives completely around. A third of the graduates go into the military, a third of them get civilian jobs of some sort, and the other third continue their education by going to college or community college. So far, the program has graduated more than 55,000 young adults who are now positive, contributing members of society, instead of a drag on it.

I know what the military has done for me and for three of my four younger brothers, and hearing the cadets' stories inspires me immensely. For many of them, the tough love of the National Guard is a tonic. After five months of boot camp, each graduate is assigned a mentor in their community who meets with them weekly to check up on how they're doing, help them set goals, and develop plans. The mentoring lasts for a full year. The program teaches these seventeen- and eighteen-year-old kids that there are causes out there more important than themselves, that they should not take for granted the blessings they have (no matter how poor they are), and that trust, respect, and teamwork come together when they accept discipline and hard work. Please think about anyone you know who might benefit from this program. It is a great, great thing. You can learn more about it at www.ngycp.org.

The other aspect of my "fame" that makes me very happy is the effect I can have on the military. Donald Trump and I did a commercial together to support recruiting efforts for the Army, Navy, Air Force, and Marines. I got to get back into uniform (yes, it was a little bigger than the one I used to wear!), do a little low-crawling in the mud, fly on a Black Hawk, and do a bit of river patrolling in a zodiac raft. The tagline for the commercial was "Once you serve in today's military, you can handle anything." And I certainly believe that is true—the impetus of this entire book is my desire to highlight the benefits of serving in the military. I couldn't be prouder of how my younger brothers have matured and become such outstanding young men, in no small part due to the training, discipline, and principles that were instilled in them by the military (even though two of them chose the Navy instead of the Army!). It's absolutely a great builder of confidence and self-esteem. I'll say it again: anyone who serves in the military gets physically fit and mentally tough—what they learn are leadership skills you just aren't going to get in any other environment.

Because of my newfound status, I was invited to visit troops at Walter Reed hospital who had been injured in Iraq. Many of them had seen episodes of *The Apprentice* before they were deployed, or watched them on tape in Iraq, and they were excited to meet me. I in turn was completely humbled in their presence. I could introduce myself to them as someone who graduated from West Point, served three years active duty, was an airborne Ranger and military intelligence officer, founded various businesses, and won *The Apprentice*. But all of those credentials were so irrelevant when I gazed at these kids who had lost part of themselves in combat.

One of the wounded at Walter Reed served as a medic in Iraq. He was getting out of his Humvee to assist wounded soldiers when an RPG hit his leg and tore it off. He tied his belt around the stump and administered first aid to troops who were lying on the ground around him, unable to move. He was hit several more times by small arms fire, and when he finished doing what he could for the other injured, he gave himself a shot of morphine, marked the time on his forehead (so whoever found him would know how to treat him properly), then finally passed out. If there is a better example of selfless service, I can't imagine it. And his was only one of many dramatic stories I heard that day.

Every single patient I met at Walter Reed had their phones right next to their beds, just waiting for a call from their unit. The sheer passion and loyalty and desire to get back to their team as soon as humanly possible literally made me cry. These kids were so fired up, so motivated, in such high spirits considering the trauma they had endured. I sat for hours after that visit thinking about those soldiers. All of us should do whatever we can to let these heroes know how much we care about them, their sacrifices, and their service.

The USO in Washington, D.C. runs this program, along with many others, for the wounded soldiers at Walter Reed. I'm a big supporter of the USO, and I hope they can continue to do their great work supporting our troops and their families.

• • •

Ross Perot on Selfless Service

I grew up in Texas during the Depression. We lived six blocks from the railroad tracks. At that time the trains were full of hobos, wandering from town to town looking for work. Every day they would come by our house looking for food. My mother would always give them something. These hobos were poor and desperate, but there was absolutely no fear that they would ever break into our house. We always left the doors unlocked.

One day, a hobo said, "Lady, don't you have a lot of people stopping by here?"

My mother replied, "Yes, we do."

He said, "Do you know why?"

She said, "Not really."

Then he took her out to our curb, showed her a mark on it, and said, "Lady, you are a mark. This says that you will feed people. That's why you get so many visitors."

After the man left, I turned to my mother and said, "Do you want me to wash that mark off the curb?"

She replied with words I will remember for the rest of my life: "No, son, leave it there. These are good people. They are just like us, but they are down on their luck. We should help them."

Pete Dawkins on Getting the Job Done

When I left the military, my first job was as head of the Public Finance Banking Department of the Wall Street firm of Lehman Brothers. After being in that position for a couple of months, I was approached by a group of veterans asking me to help in a project to erect a memorial to the Vietnam veterans of New York City. The effort was timed to correspond with the ten-year anniversary of the departure of U.S. troops from Vietnam. They asked me to be the fund chairman. It sounded like something I ought to do, so I said yes.

Right away, however, I realized the folly of my compulsiveness. I realized that I had signed on to raise a significant amount of money—several million dollars—in an extraordinarily short period of time: about 12 weeks, to be precise. And the point was, I didn't know anybody in New York; had never lived in New York; had never worked in New York, and had no contacts or "chits" to call in.

I began to madly scurry about, trying to figure out how to accomplish this task. I realized very quickly that there was no possible way to reach our goal without figuring out some way to get some "big chunks" of cash to get the ball rolling. After an emergency "brainstorming session" that lasted late into the night, the idea was floated that maybe we could get Donald Trump to give us a million dollars. It was pretty obviously a long shot, but with no better idea, we decided to press ahead.

It turns out that one of the veterans who was working with us had done a number of real estate-related, multi-media presentations for Trump. These were coordinated, computer-driven presentations that included a couple of film projectors and twelve 35-mm slide projectors all integrated together. A pretty antiquated mechanism by today's standards, but in those days it represented cutting-edge technology. We charged him to develop an emotional 3–4 minute presentation that would portray the "abandonment" of the Vietnam Veterans and, hopefully, would resonate with someone like Trump.

It took a week or so to prepare the presentation and, when it was ready, I called Donald Trump, introduced myself, and asked for an appointment to come by and talk with him. I didn't mention what it was about. To my surprise, he said "fine," and we agreed to a time. A day later, I walked into his office, shook his hand, chatted for a couple of minutes, and said, "There's something I'd like you to see. It's set up down in your screening room." He was a bit taken back, but down we went. We sat down and I explained that I had signed on to be the fund chairman for a memorial for Vietnam veterans in New York City. "I'd like to ask you for a million dollars," I said. He just sat there, and looked at me.

The room went dark and the multi-media presentation was played. I must say, it was poignantly—and powerfully—done.

A series of striking still photos of faces and places, interspersed with film of combat and medical evacuation helicopters, all set to the melodic but mournful song, "The Long and Winding Road."

When the lights came back on, there was silence. I had known Donald Trump now for all of about 14 minutes. We both sat there for what seemed like a very long time, him looking straight ahead, saying nothing. Then he turned to me and said, "OK, you've got yourself a deal." Simple as that. No big discussion. No theatrics. Just, done. He did add one condition. He said, "There's only one thing—I want to make it a challenge. We'll call it the 'Trump Challenge.' If you raise a million dollars, I'll match it."

With that commitment as the foundation, our small group of veterans went about the task of raising a million dollars. With a lot of help and support, we were able to do so in short order. We ended up raising several million dollars and, with Trump's million on top, we not only funded the memorial, but set up a permanent mentoring and employment program for NYC veterans.

Some may remember the glorious parade in New York City, where 80,000 veterans from all over the country came to march and to dedicate the memorial. It was a very touching moment that many credit with beginning the process of putting to rest the troubled sentiments of our nation about the Vietnam era. It wouldn't have been possible without being willing to take a chance on a "long shot."

TAKE COMMAND: SELFLESS SERVICE

Marty Evans said, "Everyone has the calling to give inside of them." Do you? There are so many ways to give back. Don't ignore that voice inside. You don't have to join the military to provide selfless service. Find something that is important to you, maybe something that reminds you of the help you got from someone on the way up. Or maybe it is something you didn't get. But get involved, volunteer, become a mentor—get out there and help somebody else. You and your company will be better for it. Your example of giving will inspire those around you and we'll all be better off.

CHAPTER TEN

Integrity: Take the Harder Right Over the Easier Wrong

When I was very small my grandma used to read a book to me by Jesse Stuart called *A Penny's Worth of Character*. It was a simple story about a boy named Shan, who lived in rural Kentucky in a much earlier, gentler time.

In the book, Shan Shelton is going to the store for his mother. If he had a dime, he could buy his favorite treat, a chocolate bar and a lemon soda pop. Shan knows that Mr. Conley, the storekeeper, pays a penny for each used burlap sack returned to the store in good condition. There are ten sacks at home, but Shan's mother tells him to take only nine to Mr. Conley, because the tenth sack has a hole in it. Shan wants a chocolate bar and lemon soda so badly that he disobeys his mother and takes the tenth sack.

As he walks to Mr. Conley's store, Shan delights in his world of morning glories and buttercups, red-headed woodpeckers and crawdads. He hides the sack with the hole in it in the middle of the pile, hoping Mr. Conley won't notice it. And sure enough, Mr. Conley overlooks it and Shan goes on his way with his candy and soda. But something is very wrong. The pop isn't very cold or refreshing and the chocolate has lost its sweetness—he can't enjoy them. Deceiving the storekeeper has taken all the enjoyment out of his favorite treat.

His mother immediately notices that something is wrong and soon finds out what happened. She sends Shan right back to the store with a brand-new sack. When he arrives, Mr. Conley has just spilled flour all over his floor because he tried to use the defective sack, and he and a friend are commiserating about the lack of values in kids today.

> Nothing is worthwhile that is not hard. You do not improve your muscle by doing the easy thing; you improve it by doing the hard thing, and you get your zest by doing a thing that is difficult, not a thing that is easy.
>
> —WOODROW WILSON

Shan gives Mr. Conley a new sack and refuses to take a penny candy for it, and also offers to bring in more sacks to make up for the ruined flour. Mr. Conley smiles at Shan and tells him that since he has been so honest, his debt is paid. And, he tells Shan, he thinks more of him than he ever has.

Now, this was just a simple little story, but it made a powerful impression on me as a kid. It was the perfect illustration, using an example I could easily understand at that age, of how I would feel if I was ever to lie, or cheat, or treat somebody dishonorably.

My father, a lifelong entrepreneur, made his living as a land developer. As the owner of his own business, he made tough decisions every day. Those decisions were always guided by a black-or-white, right-or-wrong attitude. There were no shades of gray for my father.

Over the years I saw his various dealings with employees, partners, and vendors. He dealt with every person and business deal from these unyielding guidelines—and he always acted with integrity. One of his favorite sayings was, "If there's a nickel in the deal he'll only take two cents and leave three cents on the table." Growing up I saw him take the harder right over the easier wrong countless times. My father would never conceal information from either partners or creditors. If something was going wrong, or a deal was proceeding more slowly than anticipated, he made sure everyone knew about it. People who worked with him were always kept fully informed. There were never any unpleasant surprises. He set a great example for me of a businessman with integrity.

When I was fifteen and competing in basketball at Central High School in Cheyenne, Wyoming, my father constantly encouraged me to remember who I was. A poem he brought to my attention more than once was called "The Man in the Glass."

> When you get what you want in your struggle for self,
> And the world makes you King for a day,
> Then go to the mirror and look at yourself,
> And see what that guy has to say.
> For it isn't your Father, or Mother, or Wife,
> Whose judgment upon you must pass.
> The fellow whose verdict counts most in your life
> Is the guy staring back from the glass.
> He's the fellow to please, never mind all the rest,

For he's with you clear up to the end,

And you've passed your most dangerous, difficult test

If the guy in the glass is your friend.

You may be like Jack Horner and "chisel" a plum,

And think you're a wonderful guy,

But the man in the glass says you're only a bum

If you can't look him straight in the eye.

You can fool the whole world down the pathway of years,

And get pats on the back as you pass,

But your final reward will be heartaches and tears

If you've cheated the man in the glass.

I learned that same lesson again at West Point, where the strict honor code was the guiding force for everything we did: "A cadet will not lie, cheat, or steal, or tolerate those who do." Now, the "not lying, cheating, or stealing" was pretty straightforward; the rest was a bit more complex. Most people would be surprised if they really thought about how often they don't quite tell the whole truth, or fudge it just a little bit, or omit something. Even if their own behavior is scrupulous, many observe lying, cheating, or stealing by others and turn away, reasoning that it isn't their problem. Even in regular daily discussions with co-workers or family, there are certain things a person might not want to come out, or would prefer to frame in a certain light. The idea behind the honor code is to reduce ambiguity, to insist on the full truth.

> Try not to become a man of success but rather try to become a man of value.
>
> —ALBERT EINSTEIN

If a cadet witnessed a violation of the West Point honor code, it was his or her duty to personally confront that person. The accused might say, "Oh no, that wasn't a crib sheet you saw me with during that test, it was something else," and produce a reasonable explanation. The whole incident might turn out to be an innocent misunderstanding. But if we believed that the honor code had been violated, we were required to turn the other cadet over to the Honor Committee or risk being charged with violating the honor code as well.

Obviously, this non-toleration clause at West Point provided a very strict rule of accountability. It is human nature to want to protect your best friend, if he swore to you that it would never happen again, and it had happened under extenuating circumstances. But the honor system is more important than the individuals involved. It defined what it meat to be a cadet and it actually made everything very simple. The rule removed all personal involvement and any potential guilt from the equation. "It looks kind of like a crib sheet and you're telling me you didn't do it? Well, I saw you do it, and I think you did it, I've got to turn you in." Boom, that's it, incident over. And is your friend really a "friend" if he or she asks you ignore that they lied, cheated, or stole something? I don't think so.

> I hope I shall always possess firmness and virtue enough to maintain what I consider the most enviable of all titles: the character of an honest man.
>
> —GEORGE WASHINGTON

Think about the ramifications of such a code in a society like ours, where so many people turn a blind eye to all kinds of misbehavior. Where CEOs of public companies say things like, "Oh, I didn't really know what was going on. No one ever told me." We are all witnessing the fallout from this lack of integrity right now. Almost every week another CEO is indicted or sent to prison because they were recklessly and selfishly running their companies in an illegal manner and completely disregarding their duty to their employees and shareholders alike. This is the price we all pay for a lack of accountability and a massive failing of both duty and integrity.

I've talked about eteamz and what a valuable business experience it was, in particular the lessons I learned from my friend Brian about passion and impeccability. I'd like to say a bit more about Steve Wynne, our CEO at eteamz when we sold it and my first true mentor in business, because he really stands out as a businessman who exemplified integrity.

At eteamz I was one of the company's first professional hires, probably about the seventh actual employee. I started off running business development, and wound up as acting president for the company. After we had raised venture capital money and angel money, we set out to recruit the very best CEO we could find. Steve Wynne had founded a law practice in Portland that now had more than a hundred employees. He had personally represented entrepreneurs. And two of the individuals he represented, Rob Strasser and Peter Moore, drove the formation of adidas America. When Rob, the CEO, passed away in 1993, Peter served as his successor until 1995, when Steve was asked, with Peter's agreement, to become CEO of adidas America while Peter became Global Creative Director. Adidas was not doing well, either in terms of image or earnings. Steve brought adidas back to both profitability and coolness.

Just one of his brilliant moves was to enter into a marketing relationship with the New York Yankees to elevate the growth of the adidas brand. You name it, he put the deal together for adidas America. He had such a sharp, great mind. He oversaw the company's turnaround and grew it back into a $1.6 billion company over a five-year period.

We were thrilled to have him on board at eteamz as our CEO. Everything he did was about being forthright and having the highest degree of personal integrity. In every company he had ever been involved with—the various business deals and boards of directors and so forth—he had brought with him this sense of integrity and honesty. It was a big part of his powerful presence and appeal. Steve was brilliant and didn't suffer fools gladly. This was a man who never dodged the tough questions. He never wanted "not to know" what was going on. It was never, "Don't tell me, and that way I won't know it is happening." The most telling aspect of that was in his dealings with our venture capitalists.

The venture capitalists we were dealing with didn't have significant experience or the depth of capital for what eteamz needed to be the leader in the market. They also lacked significant operational experience. They had been consultants, and part of running a company is having your butt on the line and making tough decisions on a P&L basis. These guys had been around it, but never in it. You find out so much about people's character when things go wrong. Everyone behaves well when everything is moving along smoothly and everyone is happy. When things go south, you see a lot of people run for the hills or covering their own butts instead of doing what's right. Roger Staubach says it a little differently: "Adversity reveals genius, while success conceals it." Meaning that, the better things are going in his organization, the more he worries about complacency and people feeling like they can coast. But when things are going badly, he can identify people who perform and who he wants in his organization for the long haul.

Things started to go badly for eteamz when the Internet bubble burst, and our two main competitors each had recently raised close to ten times the amount of money we had. Though we had the most traffic and the best product, we were not generating any revenue. We knew we had a valuable asset, but we just hadn't gotten to the point of profitability. Our venture capitalists urged us to increase our marketing budget and maintain a full staff, and promised that they would keep us solvent. But we weren't willing to have our employees work for a promise. Steve told the venture capitalists, "Listen, if you don't wire the money right now, we are firing everyone that we can't afford to pay." This was a tough decision. We had built a culture of loyalty at eteamz. Our employees knew the management team would act with integrity—and the same was expected of each of them. So, in addition to following the letter of the law (you can't allow employees to continue working if you don't have the money to pay them and payroll taxes), we were upfront with the employees. We explained the situation and said that forty of our fifty employee positions would have to be cut.

> Our character... is an omen of our destiny, and the more integrity we have and keep, the simpler and nobler that destiny is likely to be.
>
> —GEORGE SANTAYANA

Steve was quite matter of fact about it. It was a simple matter of honesty, integrity, and the law. When the Internet bubble burst, there were plenty of companies that made false promises and compromised their integrity. That option never crossed Steve's mind. The venture capitalists, to their credit, did wire some money; however, we eventually made the difficult decision to cut the staff from fifty to about a dozen people. And you know what? Almost every single employee asked to continue working at eteamz with no pay in hopes that we'd be able to raise more money. Because they believed in our vision and the team we had put together. Every single person wanted to continue trying to make the company a success. Like I said, it was a great place to work.

During our negotiations with Active (the company to which we sold eteamz) we hired a team of lawyers, one of whom was gunning for partner of his firm. Steve had made me the point person in charge of closing the deal. The lawyer contacted the buyer, Active, without our knowledge or permission and tried to negotiate pay for himself and his firm. He even took our response to an Active offer and changed it without our knowledge. Steve directed me to fire the firm in the middle of the deal and have all the records delivered to our office. And I did. Not everyone operates with integrity—and you don't want to do business with those who don't.

I was lucky to be able to work with Steve Wynne while at eteamz. He epitomized a businessman who lived by the West Point honor code and provided a great example for me to emulate.

Integrity is who you are. And integrity in business means focusing on more than building personal wealth. It's about a functioning organization with solid values—honesty, loyalty, industry—that rewards investors and gives customers a valuable product or service.

The principle of integrity is central to who Roger Staubach is. We had a long talk about the concept, and he told me, "Years before I retired from the Dallas Cowboys I founded the Staubach Company, and we started growing it in the early 1980s. It's quite a large operation now. I've enjoyed building the company. I have not been involved at all in commissions since the very early years. I have taken a lot of pleasure in seeing our people be successful and do the right thing while they are representing me and my company. My name is on the door, but this company has been built by people who have committed to the values of my company. The people who don't have these values don't last. Today the customer wants a service business. They want people they can trust who will partner with them to satisfy their real estate objectives, and that trust is so important. If we do our job in their best interests, we're going to get paid for it.

> Real integrity is doing the right thing, knowing that nobody's going to know whether you did it or not.
>
> —OPRAH WINFREY

"We have three main areas of our company: office, industrial, and retail. Now a retail customer wants more of a solution, so we do retail development. But we don't handle office and industrial development, because we don't want the conflict of ownership. This is not to say you can't do it, but the fewer conflicts you have in life, the better off you are. I want to avoid even the possibility of an appearance of a conflict of interest.

"Integrity is trust. It's making sure you live up to your commitments. Our company guarantees our services—and that guarantee is not a marketing tool. It's a major commitment. If our customer sees that we're not doing our job in any way, shape, or form, they have the option to change our compensation or they can fire us. In our industry a lot of people come to us who have signed contracts with brokers, and they can't get out of them. We don't do that because it makes our people committed to doing the right thing for our customers and our company. It's not just something we can show our customers we're going to do, it's something internally that our people have committed to. If you work for the Staubach Company, you make that commitment. And hopefully that adds value to our service.

"I'm always amazed at the complicated contracts and the amount of litigation that goes on between brokers and their customers. You'll never see that in our company."

Wow. Roger Staubach walks his talk. He has more than 1,300 employees and he still operates the same way he did in the Navy. The same way he did on the football field. A person's word is their bond. It defines who they are and what they are made of. There is no substitute, and he has built a company founded on that principle.

I continue to learn more about real estate every day in my new job at the Trump Organization. Real estate, especially in New York City, is one of the toughest industries imaginable. But the bottom line is this: banks are notoriously stingy about lending money. They only want to deal with people they know are going to pay them back. Based on Donald Trump's name and integrity, he was able to turn himself around at a time when everyone had written him off. He remains a man of great integrity, and his projects reflect that. I would not consider working anywhere, for anyone, without integrity.

I learned quite a bit about condominium sales when I got involved with Trump Tower Tampa. Whenever a developer pre-sells units in a condominium, he bases the initial sales price on what he thinks the market will bear, plus the costs of delivering the building. Because of the nature of the building trade, there are always significant changes during construction for which someone must assume the risks. Recently, the cost of oil, and therefore gasoline, has shot so high that the costs of transporting concrete, steel—all of those materials necessary to construct a building—have also skyrocketed.

A buyer who is interested in purchasing a condominium generally puts 5 to 10 percent down on the total price of the anticipated sales price in the form of a reservation. It is considered earnest money to indicate serious interest. The buyer can pull out of this commitment at any time. Much later, when the building is nearing completion, the builder says to the developer, "Here's the final cost of everything that I will commit to on this building." As soon as that figure is accounted for, the developer can adjust the sales price before going to "contract" with everyone who has a reservation.

The developer then tells the people with reservations, "The unit you are interested in is no longer selling for $500,000. Because of price fluctuations during the building process, the purchase price is now $625,000." The potential buyers have the right to back out.

The developer, of course, needs to make a profit, but if he prices the building too high—after the costs are accounted for—he can lose the sale entirely or gain a reputation as a price gouger. The proper balance is to simply be fair. If costs have risen and a new mall is being constructed near your project—which will increase the value of the building considerably—just make sure the potential buyer is kept informed. Clear communication is vital. It's the difference between acting with integrity, and acting without.

I think a real problem many people have in all kinds of businesses is that they are afraid to deliver bad news—to their boss, to clients, and to customers. The pressure keeps building and building until they feel they have no choice but to not tell the truth about something. Typically, lies or misinformation will come out, and whatever news a person did not want to impart will definitely be revealed eventually. From a short-term perspective, lying or concealing facts might help you on one certain deal. But you get a reputation as a liar and the trust that your business requires is gone.

I will not work with or do business deals with people or firms who have a reputation for being dishonest. Life is too short. Not only am I increasing my own likelihood of being taken advantage of and led down a treacherous path, I just don't have time for people who won't live up to what they say they'll do, and I don't want to be tarnished by their behavior. As a friend of mine is fond of saying, "You can only lose your good reputation once." Don't ever take that risk!

• • •

Pete Dawkins on Doing What's Right

You know, it's interesting. There's a particular experience I've had that's been almost exactly the same in a number of different leadership positions I've held—in the military, in sports, in the government, and in business. A person comes up to me and says, "I have this dilemma. I really don't know what the right thing to do is."

They then begin to explain a complex set of circumstances and behaviors that faces them with this seemingly irresolvable dilemma. Sometimes the saga is long and Byzantine. My reaction is short and simple. I steadfastly refuse to even attempt to pick apart the details, or assess motives or intentions. I simply tell them, "Look. Just do what's right."

I recognize that you might consider my response to be calloused, or simplistic—or simply unresponsive. But I don't think so. I've found that, almost invariably, the problem is *not* that the person doesn't know what the right thing to do is. The problem is that they don't *want* to have to do it! Why? Because it's a tough decision. It may hurt someone's feelings. Someone they care about. It may be short-term wise, but long-term irresponsible. It may put them in a bad light in the eyes of someone who has power over them. The fact is there are thousands of decisions we all confront where there's no "easy" answer. No "magically perfect" answer. No simple, clear, tidy, effortless, answer—without consequence or repercussion.

I'm convinced that when you really take a step back, and honestly think through all the facts and circumstances, it's almost always the case that—if you trust your gut—you do know what the right thing to do is. Then it just remains for you to decide whether you're willing to do it, or not.

TAKE COMMAND: INTEGRITY

Ultimately, you are only as good as your word. When you tell someone that you're going to do something, do it. If you can be successful at just this one thing, then you'll be way ahead of the game. It is nearly impossible to regain your integrity if you lose it. Your troops or your employees will never forget it if you compromise yourself. What's more, you'll be setting an example and they'll think it is okay. In business and in life, if those people around you are able to believe you and take you at your word, then you'll be successful. Always take the harder right over the easier wrong!

In Closing

Every task on *The Apprentice* was extremely challenging, but the bottom line was that I was in my element the whole time. I was used to being tested, graded, and ranked in public from my West Point days. Throw on top of that the fact that I had been through Ranger school, where I had been evaluated on limited sleep in a very stressful environment, surrounded by a bunch of very aggressive people. I had been trained as an Army officer to take command and lead. As Pete Dawkins said, "A leader is someone who moves people to action." I was more than ready for the challenge.

There was no privacy on the show, which freaked a lot of the other contestants out. No big deal to me—shared eating space, shared restroom facilities—it was the Army all over again, but this time it was a nice suite in Trump Tower! I wasn't sleeping on the ground in the freezing cold avoiding spiders. I truly loved the whole process—it brought out every one of my principles, from teamwork to passion to duty. There were so many proxies and parallels to what had happened in the military for me to draw on that it was completely familiar territory.

I took a lot of flak for being on the computer all the time, but every one of our tasks was massively complex. The meticulous planning and tracking of every penny we spent and the overall accounting was a big reason my teams were successful. I insisted that we lay out an operating procedure and an after-action review for every task, just like in the Army, which was key to our success. Not all of that came through to the viewers, but it was a powerful factor behind the scenes.

I felt pretty confident going into the final night of *The Apprentice*, which was broadcast live from Lincoln Center in New York City. I had put everything I had into winning, and I had one last chance to convince Donald Trump that I was the best choice. I wasn't about to change my strategy. It had worked so far, and it was very simple: I lived every day according to my ten principles. I believed in letting my actions speak for themselves, without engaging in any of the backstabbing and infighting that sometimes occurred in the board room. My opponent and I both summed up the reasons why we should be chosen. I cited my military background, my business experience, my study of law, my desire to win, and the fact that over the course of the fifteen-week show I had led my team to victory as the project manager an unprecedented four times and had won more tasks than any other *Apprentice* contender.

Being chosen as the new apprentice kicked off an intense media tour that began twenty minutes after the show ended and didn't stop for several weeks. I was at the center of a sudden whirlwind of activity—it seemed that everybody in the world wanted to interview me and know what it was like to compete and win on *The Apprentice*. I appeared everywhere from the *Today Show* to the *Tonight Show*. When I was standing onstage next to Jay Leno, I knew my life had really changed!

And has it ever changed. Just a little more than a year ago I was president of an outsource software company living in San Diego; now I live in the heart of New York City and have taken on the biggest business challenges of my life. Donald offered me the choice of New York or Las Vegas, and I immediately chose to relocate to New York after my win, because I wanted to get as close as possible to my new boss and the other key players in his organization. In New York, I would be able to interact with Donald Trump on a weekly, or even daily basis, learn his organization better, and have more hands-on access to all the projects with which he was involved. I wanted to take advantage of my new network. I felt strongly that to take advantage of this apprenticeship I needed to "sit at the feet of the master" and really see him operate. It has been one of the most rewarding business experiences of my career.

All of the rewards that have come to me for living by my ten principles have been simply amazing. The doors that are opening for me are unlimited. My network has increased exponentially, and it will allow me to do even greater things in the future. I'm very thankful to Donald Trump and his organization for allowing me these opportunities. As I write this in the close of 2005 we are just about to launch Trump Direct Media, the perfect culmination of all my business skills, and I couldn't be more excited. And I'm sure there will be more businesses in my future.

Now I want to do everything in my power to increase opportunities for other veterans. I hope that I've made a convincing case in this book that hiring men and women who have served in the military is one of the smartest decisions any employer—whether it be a huge corporation or a small local business—can make. The men and women who have served in our military have taken my ten principles to heart, which I feel is essential to success in any endeavor. And I hope this book will inspire veterans to go out and conquer the business world.

I know what living by these ten principles has done for me, and I'd like to hear from you, my readers, about how they've helped you. I spoke with six amazing leaders for this book. But I know there are plenty more out there. So please send your personal stories that show how any one of the ten principles has worked for you. I'd love to put them on my website. There are so many inspiring examples out there—whether they come from the military, work, or just regular daily life, and whether they come from CEOs or privates in the Army. I'd love to share them with the world. Check out the forums at www.kellyperdew.com for details. Who knows, maybe you'll be a contributor to my next book!

Acknowledgments

First of all, I accept 100 percent responsibility for any omissions or misstatements of fact contained within these pages. All errors are due wholly to my lack of attention to detail. Additionally, I want to make it clear that any particularly witty or persuasive/poignant writing found herein is, in all likelihood, due to an external contributor.

My first acknowledgment goes to my first hero—H.T. "Hub" Perdew, my grandfather, who passed away at 100 years old in March 2005 prior to my writing this book. But he did see the show. Thanks, Grandpa. You instilled many of the values that exist in our family, and thank you, Dad, for reinforcing them. Both of you have been heroes to me and set a tremendous path for me to follow.

I am lucky to have four younger (all of them bigger) brothers, who keep me on my toes and make me prouder every day. I'm constantly learning from each of you and hope I can provide you with even a little of what you provide me. Hal, you especially inspire me and I thank you for motivating me to throw my hat in the ring for *The Apprentice*.

I owe a tremendous debt of gratitude to all the people I served with in the military; especially Andy Hergenrother, who exemplified every principle in this book. I salute you, sir. And to all of you servicemen and women out there—Hooo Ahhhh!

I am so privileged to have spent time with the distinguished contributors to my book: Bill Coleman, Pete Dawkins, Marty Evans, Jim Kimsey, Ross Perot, and Roger Staubach. Each of you generously shared your time to discuss how the leadership principles learned in the military shaped your approach to business. Thank you again.

I thank you, Donald Trump and Mark Burnett, for creating a medium that allowed me to display these principles for an audience of millions. The Trump organization is a great place to work and you have all been incredibly generous in welcoming me with open arms. Thank you Donald, George, Carolyn, Norma, Bernie, Cathy, Sid, Courtney, Jeff, Sonya, Jen, and Steve—I've learned a lot from all of you!

Jon Kraft, my longtime friend and business partner, you supported me in this *Apprentice* endeavor from the very beginning and I credit you with the title for this book.

Putting this book together required a Herculean effort and I, luckily, had a great team. Thank you, Regnery, especially Marji Ross, Jeff Carneal, and Ben Domenech, for believing in me; my tenacious literary agent, Sharlene Martin; my publicists at Levine Communications; and Julie McCarron, who helped me take all these ideas and make them intelligible. I couldn't ask for a more professional and inspired team. Rock on!

A special thanks to Rick Levy, my good friend of some ten-plus years and the chief operating officer at ICM (definitely a good guy to know if you ever win a reality show!). I know you're always there for me and I thank you from the bottom of my heart.

Kassie, you are what I feel most lucky about in my life. Thank you for supporting me and sharing in this incredible adventure.

Finally, to all the servicemen and women protecting us—thank you.

Index

A

accountability: duty and, 15, 16, 26–27; integrity and, 181

Active.com, 42, 43, 44, 45–46, 185

Adams, John Quincy, 71

Addison, Joseph, 82

adidas, 41, 182–83

Aetna, 87

Afghanistan, 20

Allen, Kevin, 40, 128

America Online (AOL), 6, 25

Anderson Business School, UCLA, 35, 37, 38, 51, 86, 104

Andy, 40

AOL. *See* America Online

AOL Foundation, 165

Apple, 95

The Apprentice, 3, 23, 25, 33, 76, 77, 193–95; duty and, 18–19; flexibility and, 147; impeccability and, 40; loyalty and, 128; military and, 193–94; passion and, 57, 58–60; perseverance and, 78; planning and, 91, 92, 99; selfless service and, 165; teaching aspect of, 49, 167–68; teamwork and, 113. *See also* Trump, Donald

Arizona Cardinals, 20

Arizona State University, 20

B

Bangalore, India, 120

Barton, Clara, 160